Return To

Mr. Thomas Nichols
RR 1 Box 89
Tallula, IL 62688-9737

D1446396

George E. Vandeman

It Is Written Classics

GEORGE E. VANDEMAN

Pacific Press Publishing Association
Boise, Idaho
Montemorelos, Nuevo Leon, Mexico
Oshawa, Ontario, Canada

Edited by Ken McFarland
Cover design by Tim Larson
Portrait of George Vandeman by Ilyong Cha
Type set in 10/12 Century Schoolbook

First Printing 1986: 5500

ISBN 0-8163-0645-1

Contents

Section I: Sometimes You Need a Prophet

Please, God, Be Careful!	7
Robots Don't Fight	13
A Strange War	17
Tears on Other Worlds	23
The Strategy of Rebellion	29
Sometimes You Need a Prophet	33
The Confounding of the Psychics	39
Decoding Bible Prophecy	47

Section II: The Rise and Fall of Antichrist in the Prophecies of Revelation

The Year 2000	55
The Day After Doomsday	63
Hitler's Last Gasp	71
Mutiny in Paradise	81
When the Red Phone Rings	89
The Antichrist Exposed	97
Bloodstained Stars and Stripes	107
Airlift From Armageddon	119

Section III: Toying With the Nick of Time

Fifteen Minutes More	127
Showdown in the Middle East	137
Identification, Please	145
The Writing on the Wall	153
The Rattle of the Keys	163
Winds on a Leash	173
Rescue From Orion	181
The Whisper of the Ax	189
Forever Marked	199
God's Yellow Ribbons	213

Before You Turn the Page

The rising crescendo of serious interest in understanding Bible prophecy is heartening. "It Is Written," through its many years of telecasting, has considered declaring the predictive portion of Scripture a priority. As this book goes to press, the scripts for "It Is Written's" most ambitious project involving prophecy have been completed and will be included under the subtitle "The Rise and Fall of Antichrist in the Prophecies of Revelation."

However, Section I on the rich background of decoding Bible prophecy will come first. Please notice how the entire Bible, from Genesis to Revelation, orchestrates Bible prophecy as a dominant and recurring theme.

"Toying With the Nick of Time" follows the Revelation segment, giving the reader an exciting survey of what the Bible has to say about the second coming of Jesus Christ, the Hope of the ages—our supreme Hope today.

Please, God, Be Careful!

An American president, speaking to an audience of women, read a letter that he had received from the mother of a U. S. serviceman. This is what it said:

"A week ago my son was still enrolled in the college of his choice. Tonight he's in a strange motel somewhere. Tomorrow he steps onto an airplane which will take him far away. He enlisted in a branch of the U. S. armed forces.

"During these past weeks I've sensed and seen him . . . in the process of pulling away, cutting the cord, getting ready to leave the nest. I saw him bequeath some valuable possessions, like his penny collection and his baseball cards. They went to a couple of small boys in his Pied Piper following on the block."

The mother said she had watched him wax his new car. And he had told her she was a great cook. And she wrote, "So I now take my place among the thousands of other mothers who through the years have watched as their feelings were not so different from mine tonight.

"Actually," she said, "It's all quite appropriate. This is a guy who grew up in a room wallpapered with flags and muskets and drums. He regularly ran Old Glory up the flagpole in the backyard before breakfast in those days. He and his big brother had G. I. Joe uniforms, sizes 4 and 6."

She went on, "I remember seeing them sneak up the little hill in the neighbor lady's backyard on their stomachs. I wonder how many times I've picked up little plastic army men from under the furniture. All those toys and memories have been packed away for years, but I feel the need to bring them out and handle them tonight.

"He has examined the options, as I suggested. The choices he's made are taking him far away from me. He believes there are opportunities for him in education, travel and experience. No doubt there are.

"He thinks he's getting a good deal. No doubt he is.

"Personally, I'm inclined to believe the country is getting a good deal. In exchange for all their provisions, they're getting one tall, tanned fellow with summer-bleached hair, a sharp young mind and more potential and possibilities than I have space to describe."

And then she concluded, "Thank you for taking the time from running the nation to listen to the passions of a mother's heart. And, please, will you be especially careful with the country just now."

The president replied solemnly, "I will be very careful with the country just now."

A mother's letter to an American president. And there were tears all over the audience. The first lady, sitting on the platform near her husband, had big tears running down her cheeks.

It's good that he was speaking to an audience of women, for men might have cried too. And men try not to cry, except when it's very dark and very still and no one is listening but God.

There's so much that is wrong with our world right now, so much that technology can't fix. It seems to be so fragile. It trembles and quakes and convulses as if about to break up. Solid earth isn't so solid anymore. It slides into the sea. It sinks into the mud. It washes away in the floods that follow the fires. It blows away. Stronger hands than those of even our best leaders are needed now.

It is no wonder that from uncounted hearts there rises like incense the silent, unspoken cry, "Please, God, be very careful with our little world!"

And with good reason. For our world really is little, so little that is seems it would never be missed if suddenly it should disappear.

Mark Twain, in his story "Captain Stormfield's Visit to

Heaven," shared a tale that was obviously intended to be completely absurd. Captain Stormfield, the story goes, had died and was on his way to heaven, but was unable to resist the temptation to race with a comet. He ended up way off course, in a sort of heavenly "missing persons bureau." An angel, wanting to help, went up in a balloon alongside a huge map of the universe, hoping to locate our solar system. The map was about the size of the whole state of Rhode Island. Three days later the angel came back down to report that he might have found our solar system, but he couldn't be sure. It might have been just flyspecks!

Just an absurd piece of exaggeration. Never intended to be taken seriously. But we know now that Mark Twain may not have been so far off. We *are* like a tiny cinder on the edge of the universe. Could the Creator ever be concerned with us? Does He even know that we are here?

It was David who wrote, "When I consider your heavens, the work of your fingers, the moon and the stars, which you have set in place, what is man that you are mindful of him, the son of man that you care for him?" Psalm 8:3, 4, NIV.

Some believe that visitors from outer space are circling the earth, looking us over, wondering about us. But the astronomer Carl Sagan discounts such an idea. He says there's nothing very interesting, nothing special about our planet. He describes it as "where the action isn't."

But our little world is so important, and so frightening, to *us*. It's so full of trouble and confusion and hate. And it's hurtling so fast, somewhere. We have a feeling that something is very wrong. We live in the atmosphere of expected crisis. Are we about to collide with something, or burn up, or explode, or perhaps be sucked into one of those black holes they talk about? What if God should drop one of those black holes? What if He should drop us?

Years ago a popular song was pleading, "Stop the world! I want to get off!" It was a clever title. Some took it seriously even then. Today we all do. If only there were some escape— somewhere to go—somewhere safe—before the planet we're riding goes up in smoke.

God said through the prophet Isaiah, "The earth will wear out like a garment." Isaiah 51:6, NIV.

And do you recall these words from the book of Revelation? "The time has come for . . . destroying those who destroy the earth." Revelation 11:18, NIV.

Does God know the trouble we're in? Does He know we're on this speeding, careening planet—and does He care? Are we on a collision course with doomsday? Can God correct our course the way NASA corrects the path of its spacecraft? And if He can— does He intend to, and in the nick of time?

NASA's *Voyager 2*, after a four-year journey from earth, reached its closest encounter with Saturn's rings right on time—almost on time. It was 2.7 seconds early! We marvel, and rightly, at such precision.

But if NASA can work such technological miracles, if NASA can boost a vehicle from here to Saturn's rings—what about the One who *made* Saturn and the incredible beauty of its rings? Is His power less than that of the people He has made?

That's another question that will have to be settled before we can sleep well at night. Did God create Saturn—and this world— and us? In the very first ten words of the Bible—the ancient and indestructible Book that claims to be the Word of God—in those very first words it says, "In the beginning God created the heavens and the earth." Genesis 1:1. NIV.

Did He—or didn't He? If He did, then we have nothing to fear. But if He didn't, then the Bible is a Book not to be trusted—and we'd better forget the idea of its being even a good book. If the Book is not what it claims to be, then it is the work of the worst impostor the world has ever known.

Yet impostor or not, the Author of the Bible puts its most incredible claim right up front, in the first ten words, making Himself vulnerable, as if to invite challenge. God stands or falls, and so does our personal security along with that of the universe, with the credibility of those ten words. For who of us can sleep peacefully tonight, believing that our future is in the hands of blind, bungling chance? Chance that, according to all the laws of probability, never created anything and never will.

This is something that has to be settled before we can face the future with any confidence at all. Do we, or do we not, have a Creator? Were we made in the image of God, as the Book says? Or are we the hapless children of some cosmic accident, of some long-buried mystery that fizzled?

How can we pray to a God who lied to us in His first ten words—if He did? Our cry is lost before it gets through the ceiling, if there is no one listening. It is a mockery to pray to One we have written off as myth, as dead, or as a liar.

"Please, God, be very careful with our little world!" Such a prayer makes sense only as we believe that He is there, that He is listening, and that He really does hold this frightened, wobbly world in His hands!

Remember the song, the old spiritual that we all love? "He's got the whole world in His hands. . . . He's got the little tiny baby in His hands. . . . He's got everybody in His hands." Remember?

But did you know that this world, and the whole human race, trembled in His hands once—for a few moments? And not a soul knew!

It was a Thursday evening. Jesus and His closest friends— eleven of them—were on their way out of the city. Eleven of them—not twelve, for one had left the group a little while earlier. Jesus had sent him on an errand, they thought. But the errand was his own. He had gone to finalize a project he had been thinking about—the betrayal of his Lord. And only Jesus knew.

It was a beautiful spring evening. The moon was bright. But something was wrong. Something was wrong with Jesus. He seemed troubled, weighted down with some terrible problem that they could not understand. He must be very tired.

Leaving the others, He took three of His men deep into the garden. He needed them to share His terrible ordeal. He needed to know that they were waiting and praying nearby. But they understood not at all what was happening. How could the Messiah, the Son of God, need their prayers? Besides, they were exhausted. Twice He came back and found them asleep.

So Jesus went on alone. And His unseen enemy was there waiting. This was his chance.

Try to forget the paintings of Gethsemane that you have seen. Jesus kneeling by a carefully chosen rock. His robe flawlessly draped. Every hair in place. Ready for the camera. No. It wasn't like that at all. Jesus was carrying the sins of the whole world that night. And the Father, though it caused Him exquisite pain to do it, must withdraw His presence from His Son. I picture Jesus falling prostrate on the cold ground, digging His fingers into the dirt as if to keep from being drawn still farther from His Father.

Jesus had come to this planet to give His life for a lost race. All His life His footsteps had been leading straight to this hour. But now it loomed like a monster before Him. Was there no other way to save men? The tempter saw His human weakness and pressed his strongest arguments. Why should He die for a world that didn't even want to be saved? Why not call for a legion of angels to sweep Him back to heaven? Let men pay for their own sins!

The fate of the whole human race trembled in the balance as Jesus wrestled with the temptation to turn back. But no. The cry of a lost and lonely planet was ringing in His ears. He would go through with the decision that had brought Him to this world. And when Judas came with the cruel mob in search of Him, He stood tall and straight, ready for the cross that now in only hours would overtake Him.

And that's why you—and I—are safe in His hands. That's why we can sleep tonight unafraid, knowing that He will be very, very careful with our little world!

Robots Don't Fight

Imagine, if you will, that you are a boy of five again, playing with toy soldiers, parading them across the floor in perfect rank. They take orders patiently, and carry them out without protest. Toy soldiers are such fun.

But tell me, little boy. What if those toy soldiers should suddenly come alive? What if suddenly they were real? Your eyes light up at the thought! Real soldiers! And they would be such good soldiers! They would still do everything you tell them. But they would be real. As real as your dog. As real as you. They could even salute you when they pass by. Not toys anymore!

But, what if it doesn't work out that way? What if one of those soldiers decides he is going to rebel? What if he sullenly refuses to march when you tell him to march? What if he wrenches his painted face into an ugly snarl and calls you a dictator?

What if those come-alive soldiers start fighting with each other, and then killing each other, until you have a full-scale war on your hands? What would you do about it?

Even at five years old you're bigger than they are. You could cuff them and force them back into line. That would prove you are still in charge.

Yes, it would prove you're in charge. But it would also prove you didn't really want them to come alive after all. You really wanted toys!

Even a child can understand that if you let your toys come alive, you take a big risk!

Now you understand God's problem! He didn't want toys that He could manipulate and control. He didn't want robots. He didn't want windup angels or battery-powered people. He didn't want His vast kingdom filled with electronic subjects that didn't even know they were being controlled. He wanted real live angels He could love—and who could love Him back. He wanted people free to choose, to love Him or not love Him—even if it meant that one of them, or all of them, should rebel.

If that should happen, of course, He could force His subjects back into line. He could throw them away like broken toys. That would prove that He had the power. But it would also prove—or seem to prove—that He hadn't really wanted subjects who could think and choose. He had wanted robots—robots who wouldn't fight. And that wouldn't be true.

Then, too, if He should throw away His people, it would appear to those looking on that there must be something harsh and cruel in His makeup. They wouldn't understand.

He could just ignore the rebellion—look the other way and pretend it hadn't happened. But if He did that, chaos would result. Rebellion would spread. His kingdom would fall.

He could try to explain the wrongness of rebellion to those looking on—so they would understand why He had to throw away the people He had made. But trying to explain the dangers of rebellion to those who had never seen it would be like trying to explain trigonometry to those tin soldiers on the floor!

So what would God do? Do you see His dilemma?

Edna St. Vincent Millay died in 1950. She was an agnostic, an unbeliever. Her words were sharp and sometimes impudent. But in one of her poems, published after her death, it is evident that she understood God's problem better than most people do. Frederick B. Speakman took the poem out of its verse form and translated it into this:

"I'm not overly impressed with the job God did in creating the world. Oh, it's amazing from where I look out at it, of course. But to turn such a trick would be routine and simple if your power were such as God's must be. To manipulate matter, this heavy, obstinate stuff He used—it's stubborn to be sure—but in such hands as God's it should have been easy and great fun to bend it into shape, to toss a planet here and set off a star there, and whip up a galaxy to fit them in, and even to concentrate on our little globe and decorate its crust with life! No," she argues, "if I had the wisdom and skill and strength of the Almighty I'm certain I could turn out a world at least as beautiful and brave, and as frightened and sorrowful as ours is.

"But that other trouble God got Himself into, that's what appalls me! To fashion the human heart, then set it free, turn it loose on its own and watch it go its way and turn all botched and bawdy and profligate, then try to win us back again to what He meant us for! To read our hearts as they are by now, these layers upon layers of wrong laminated in our souls like the leaves that are pressed into coal, and then try to disentangle all that without forcing us! To understand all that without hating us! To punish our wrongs without utterly destroying us! And still to keep trying to persuade our kind of wickedness to choose His kind of goodness.

"There's the real trouble," she concludes. "I can't understand why He bothered in the first place, and I don't see for a moment how anything much can ever come of it. But how I respect Him for daring to try!" *Love is Something You Do*, pp. 35, 36.

Could a believer have said it better? Perhaps not—except that the believer knows that God will yet succeed, with enough human hearts to make it worth the trouble!

And we, too, though much may seem dark and mysterious now, will one day understand—and say it was worth it all!

The mystery of evil, even now, is not locked away from us. It is not an impenetrable secret. We can know both the origin and the outcome of rebellion against God. We can know who the opponents are and what the issues are in this conflict between good and evil. We may not understand the why of every brush with trouble. But we are not left to float like corks on an ocean, without sail or ballast or destination.

"The secret things belong to the Lord our God," said Moses, "but the things revealed belong to us and to our children forever." Deuteronomy 29:29, NIV.

And more things have been revealed than you would ever dream!

A Strange War

What kind of weapons would you expect God to use if He should be involved in a war? Certainly He would not bother with such primitive weapons as spears or guns or conventional bombs. Most certainly He who made the atom must understand all the intricacies of its possible behavior. Nuclear power would be at His instant command. For that matter, He who spoke worlds into existence (Psalm 33:6, 9) could easily speak His enemies out of existence.

But the book of Revelation tells us that there *was* a war in heaven. And there is something very strange about that war, for there is no mention whatever of weapons. And stranger still, there was not even one fatality on either side. Listen to this:

"And there was war in heaven. Michael and his angels fought against the dragon, and the dragon and his angels fought back. But he was not strong enough, and they lost their place in heaven. The great dragon was hurled down—that ancient serpent called the devil or Satan, who leads the whole world astray. He was hurled to the earth, and his angels with him." Revelation 12:7-9, NIV.

Not a shot was fired. Not a spear thrust. Not a bomb dropped. No death ray. And not a single fatality. Satan and his angels lost the war. They were simply thrown out, banished from heaven. No longer was heaven their home.

At this moment every participant in that war is still alive. Not one of the losers is now behind bars. All have a frightening

17

measure of freedom, though God has placed some restrictions upon their activities.

Strange? We shall discover why!

We shall discover that this war in heaven was only the beginning of an agelong controversy that is not yet finished. But when it *is* finished, when there is not one in all the universe who will misunderstand God's dealing with rebellion, it will not be like the beginning. No issue will be left undecided. God will no longer need to place Himself on trial before His subjects. His character will never again be questioned. And in the final confrontation, here on this planet, on one side no casualties, and, on the other side, no survivors. Rebellion will be over forever—and with it all the heartache it has caused!

It may seem that God is slow to intervene. But remember—He is taking time to do it right. Would you want it otherwise?

But now back to this strange war in heaven. Who were the participants? Michael and His angels. The dragon and his angels. The dragon is identified as the ancient serpent, the devil, or Satan. The devil and Satan are of course one and the same. And it is appropriate also to call him the ancient serpent, for it was disguised as a serpent that he maneuvered the downfall of our first parents.

But who is Michael? Evidently—or Michael the archangel (Jude 9)—is none other than the Son of God, the One we know as Christ or Jesus.

But someone says, "Wait! Jesus wasn't born until Bethlehem. And wasn't this a long time before Bethlehem?"

Yes. But the prophet Micah, in predicting the birth of Jesus in Bethlehem (Micah 5:2), tells us that the One to be born there had existed "from everlasting." And according to the apostle John (John 1:1, 14), there never was a time when the One we call Jesus did not exist along with His Father.

Jesus was not a created being. He was not an angel. He was not an angel elevated to a higher position—He was God! The apostle Paul (in Hebrews 1:3-14) makes this crystal clear. Jesus is sometimes called the archangel (compare Jude 9 with 1 Thessalonians 4:16 and John 5:28, 29) not because He was an angel, but because He was the loved Commander of the angels.

It is interesting that the name Michael in the Scriptures seems to be used primarily, if not exclusively, in speaking of the conflict between the Son of God and Satan. It seems reasonable, then, that Michael may have been the name by which Jesus was known in heaven before He was born in Bethlehem.

In that war in heaven, then, Michael and His loyal angels were arrayed against Satan and his angels—the angels who sided with him in his rebellion.

And now someone is saying, "Who are the angels? Aren't they the spirits of people who have died here in our world?"

No. That could hardly be the case, for angels were in existence long before ever this earth was created—long before any one had died. Angels are the beings created to inhabit heaven —the world where God's throne is.

But now we must identify Satan more specifically, for it is important that we understand just who the characters are in this agelong conflict. What is the background of this leader of rebellion? Who was he before he was called Satan, before he became the devil, before he rebelled? Certainly God did not create a devil. It is unthinkable that there should be a devil factory in heaven. What happened?

The prophet Isaiah identifies the author of rebellion as "Lucifer, son of the morning." See Isaiah 14:12.

Son of the morning! Only a brilliant angel would have such a title. But something happened. A change came about. The brilliant son of the morning became a devil—made of himself a devil—and fell from heaven.

The prophet gives us some details. "How art thou fallen from heaven, O Lucifer, son of the morning! . . . Thou hast said in thine heart, I will ascend into heaven, I will exalt my throne above the stars of God: . . . I will ascend above the heights of the clouds; I will be like the most High." Isaiah 14:12-14, KJV.

It all started in the heart, in the mind, where all wrong begins. This brilliant being became dissatisfied with being an angel, even the highest angel. He coveted the throne of God. He wanted to be like God—in power, but not in character.

The prophet Ezekiel has recorded for us the words spoken by God to Lucifer: "Thou art the anointed cherub that covereth;

and I have set thee so: thou wast upon the holy mountain of God. . . . Thou wast perfect in thy ways from the day that thou wast created, till iniquity was found in thee. . . . Thine heart was lifted up because of thy beauty, thou hast corrupted thy wisdom by reason of thy brightness." Ezekiel 28:14-17, KJV.

Do you get the picture? This brilliant angel, so honored that he stood next to the throne of God, became proud of his beauty, proud of his brightness, and began to think that even as heaven's highest angel he was not honored enough. He was loved and adored by the other angels, but that seemed not enough. He wanted unlimited power, unlimited control. He didn't want to be an angel at all. He wanted to be God!

Evidently Lucifer didn't resist these thoughts. On the contrary, he encouraged them. And there, in the heart of the son of the morning, sin entered the universe. It had never existed before. And no one but God—because He knows all things—knew what sin was or how lethal it would be.

Sin is mysterious. It cannot be explained, for to explain it would be to excuse it, and it cannot be excused. Lucifer could not plead that he was deprived, that he was discriminated against, or that his environment was to blame. Heaven had given him everything it had to give. But he wanted more!

At first he may not have understood the strange feelings in his heart. But certainly the issues were explained to him. Tenderly the Son of God must have pleaded with him to turn back. Loyal angels must have urged him not to continue his fearful course. At that point he could have turned back and been forgiven. But he was too proud to repent. He began to spread his discontent among the angels until a third of them had sided with him (Revelation 12:4). Dissatisfaction turned to open revolt, to open rebellion. Lucifer, son of the morning, had become the devil. And he, along with his angels-turned-demons, was banished from heaven.

Was God in any way responsible for all this? Was this brilliant angel created with some hidden flaw? Had God, even unwittingly, created a devil? Never! God does nothing unwittingly. And God does nothing imperfectly. Lucifer, we read a few moments ago, was perfect from the day he was created. Remember?

Created perfect. But not created a robot. He was created with the power to choose. To him had been given the dangerous gift of freedom. God knew the risk He took. He knew that sometime, somewhere, someone might choose to sin, choose to rebel. And Lucifer did.

What would God do now? Destroying Lucifer and his angels would be misunderstood. It would appear to support the rebel charge that God was arbitrary and cruel—a tyrant who had no love for His subjects. The plant of sin must be allowed to grow until all the universe should see its deadly bloom. The character of Satan must be unmasked. God must place Himself on trial before His subjects and let them see who it is that cares.

It would take time—millenniums of time. But there was no other way. For if a trace of rebellion remained, if in even one mind there remained a question about God's character, it would one day rise to threaten the security of the universe again. Men and angels and watching worlds must see the horrible lengths to which sin would go. They must see demonstrated again and again the ruthless, lying, uncaring nature of sin. They must see enough of it—so much of it—in all its shameful reality—that the whole universe will turn away in settled horror—never to touch it again!

Was there no way that all this could have been prevented? Was the tragedy of sin inevitable? Did rebellion have to happen?

No. It didn't have to happen. God had a number of options. He could have filled the universe with empty worlds, with galaxies without a spark of life, with stars that spin obediently in their orbits because they cannot do otherwise. But stars could not worship. Stars could not love. Empty worlds could not heal the loneliness in the heart of a loving God. Galaxies, no matter how dazzling their brilliance, could bring no joy to worlds where not a single eye was turned their way.

How could a God of love, His heart bursting with the urge to share—how could such a God be satisfied with a vast, lifeless, untouched emptiness all about Him? How could such a God be silent when He knew that the sound of His voice could call the limitless, silent wilderness of space to life?

He could, of course, fill his kingdom with robots programmed to obey and worship and even to talk of love. But God would not be fooled by His own creation. True, there would be no risk. Rebellion would be impossible. But so would happiness and satisfaction and peace and joy. God would still be lonely.

If the Creator, knowing all things, knew who would rebel, then He could have called to life only those He knew would be loyal subjects. He could leave uncreated anyone who would ever disturb the peace of the universe. But would that be true freedom? Would such a manipulation of creation be any more excusable than manipulating the minds and choices of His subjects? Hardly! How could God be happy knowing that the universe was secure only because He squelched even the possibility of rebellion by leaving all rebels unborn?

There was one more option. God could place within every created one the power to choose, to be loyal or not to be loyal. The risk was tremendous but the possibilities were fantastic. He took the risk. He created angels, and heaven rang with song. He filled the spinning worlds with the happy sounds of life.

Worlds, did I say? Life on other worlds? Yes, I believe there is!

Tears on
Other Worlds

According to a somewhat dubious legend, a distinguished astronomer, many years ago, received a message from the famed newspaper tycoon William Randolph Hearst, the father of today's publisher Randolph Hearst. The message read:

IS THERE LIFE ON MARS? CABLE THOUSAND WORDS. HEARST

The astronomer replied, as requested, in a thousand words. It was simply "NOBODY KNOWS," repeated five hundred times!

We've come a long way since then. And we've gone a long way, 230 million miles, to land *Viking* on Mars. Is there life there? That was the question in everybody's mind. Scientists watched breathlessly as the evidence seemed to teeter between "Yes, there is" and "No, there isn't."

Presumably, even if Mr. Hearst's question were extended to include the whole universe rather than simply Mars, astronomers would still answer, "NOBODY KNOWS."

But is that true? Doesn't anybody know? Can't we know?

I don't want to appear presumptuous. But on the basis of what I have read in God's Book, I can say, "Yes, Mr. Hearst, there *is* life on other worlds."

Now the Bible doesn't say in so many words that other worlds are inhabited by intelligent life. But if I were a detective looking for evidence, I'd certainly consider a number of Bible statements mighty hot clues. Listen to this:

"For thus saith the Lord that created the heavens; God himself that formed the earth and made it; he hath established it,

23

he created it not in vain, he formed it to be inhabited." Isaiah 45:18, KJV.

God intended this planet to be the home of life. And since it *is* the home of life, its creation was not in vain. Does this not mean that if God's other worlds were uninhabited, they would have been created in vain—useless? That's the clear implication.

Think it through. Is it reasonable to believe that God would create billions upon billions of worlds and fit only one of them up with people?

Here is another significant scripture: "Thou, even thou, art Lord alone; thou hast made heaven, the heaven of heavens, with all their host . . . ; and the host of heaven worshippeth thee." Nehemiah 9:6, KJV.

These words suggest to me that the universe is teeming with life, intelligent life, intelligent enough to worship. And all worship God. They are loyal subjects of His kingdom. They haven't rebelled as this one unruly planet has.

But now listen to this: "God . . . hath in these last days spoken unto us by his Son, . . . by whom also he made the worlds." Hebrews 1:1, 2, KJV.

"His Son, . . . by whom he made the worlds"—plural. More than one world. Many worlds. There may be billions of worlds. And who made them? Our Lord Jesus Christ. "God, who created all things by Jesus Christ." Ephesians 3:9, KJV.

Is this a surprise? Christ—the One we know as Jesus—made the worlds? He made all things? Yes. The apostle John, in his first chapter, leaves no room for confusion on this point. He says in verse 10, concerning Jesus, "He was in the world, and the world was made by him, and the world knew him not." And in verse 3, he says, "All things were made by him; and without him was not anything made that was made." KJV.

Do you see what this means? It means not only that the One we know as Jesus existed from eternity with His Father. It means also that Jesus created the worlds, including our world. And if He made our world, He made man. He is our Creator—yours and mine.

It means, too, that Jesus created the angels—including Lucifer. Lucifer was not rebelling against the rule of a fellow angel. He was rebelling against his own Creator!

You see, in the early days of Lucifer's dissatisfaction, this planet existed only in the minds and planning of the Father and the Son. The unhappy angel knew that he was to have no part in its creation. And now we have touched the very core of his disaffection.

The Son of God had created many worlds. Lucifer had created none. And now the Father and the Son were planning still another world, and Lucifer had not been invited into their counsel. Why? Why should he not have the same privileges as the Son? If God alone could create, if an angel could never create, then Lucifer didn't want to be an angel. He wanted to be God!

Jesus was divine. He was God. He was the Creator. An angel was none of these, nor could ever be. God explained it all carefully and tenderly to the dissenter. But it only enraged him. His jealousy knew no bounds. He wanted the place of the Son of God. He would be satisfied with nothing less. His dissatisfaction was spreading, threatening to become open revolt.

Would the Father and the Son now abandon their plan to create this earth—because of the Lucifer problem? No! They would go ahead. And there was something special about this creation. For they would create man in their own image. Evidently man was to more nearly resemble his Creator, in appearance and in character, than any of the beings previously created.

So it was that the One we call Jesus, with His Father, sped through the galaxies to this lonely spot in the universe, called a world into existence, flung it into space, and set it spinning. It was He, the One we call Jesus, who said, "Let there be light." It was He who spent nearly a week in making this planet a place of unscarred beauty, fitting it up as if for a king. See Genesis 1 and 2.

And now it was Friday afternoon. The garden He had planted pleased Him. The trees were there, casting their lacy shadows in the sunlight. The fruit was ripe and ready to eat. The animals were playing together. The birds were singing. The sound of a waterfall gave it the final touch. Everything was ready. The moment had come.

And the One we call Jesus knelt down and fashioned a body out of the unmarred soil. When it was complete and perfect, every part of it ready to function at the divine signal, He breathed life into the body. See Genesis 2:7. And Adam opened his eyes to see the face of his Creator, the first face he had ever seen.

I don't know what Jesus said to Adam. Someone has suggested that Jesus just smiled and said, "Hi, Adam!"

I like that. What a happy moment! What a happy day! What a time for singing! No wonder "the morning stars sang together, and all the sons of God shouted for joy"! Job 38:7, KJV.

It would seem that such a day could not hold any more happiness. But it did. Jesus permitted Adam to become drowsy and fall asleep. And when he opened his eyes again he saw beside him the most beautiful woman in the world. Not because she was the *only* woman in the world, but because Jesus Himself had fashioned her.

Then as the sunlight began to fade, Adam and Eve watched their first sunset together, with their Creator beside them. What a moment to remember!

At that sunset hour the sixth day of Creation week was ending, and the seventh day beginning. The work of creation was finished, and God saw that it was "very good."

What would God do now? Would He hurry back to the comfort of heaven and His throne, to enjoy the adoration of the angels? Would He turn now to other projects, giving His attention to other galaxies and other worlds, forgetting the happy couple He had made? Would He leave them to speculate about how they got here? No. He chose to spend that first Sabbath with His newest creation.

I picture Him slipping back to Adam and Eve for an evening walk as the stars came out, telling them about those lights in the sky and how He had made them too. They had so many questions, so much that they wanted to know. In the morning they must have walked and talked with Him again. How they wished that the day would never end! And how thrilled they were when the Creator told them that this happy, unforgettable day could be repeated—each seventh day, as it rolled around, could be a time of special fellowship with Him.

We are told that "on the seventh day God ended his work which he had made; and he rested on the seventh day from all his work which he had made." Genesis 2:2, KJV.

I confess that there is something in that scripture that is difficult to understand. How could God rest, truly rest, no matter how successful the week had been—how could He rest when He knew that all was not well in heaven? How could He rest, knowing that the universe had been contaminated by the virus of rebellion? Especially, how could He rest knowing that the happy pair He had just created might someday rebel? It could happen. He had given them the dangerous gift of freedom to choose.

And yet God rested—the Father and the Son. Rested because in counsel together They had agreed upon a plan. Rested because in the heart of the One we call Jesus, Calvary lay hidden!

Lucifer's dissatisfaction had now become open revolt. And revolt became war. And Lucifer became Satan, the fallen angel. And Satan, with his sympathizers, was banished from heaven.

The Father and the Son must have wept together that day. For They had lost not only a brilliant and beloved angel, the highest of them all, but They had lost a great host of angels that Lucifer had led into revolt. The loyal angels must have silenced their harps and wept too. And the unfallen worlds, as they watched, must have joined in Their tears.

There was a great emptiness now in God's world. And the emptiness would remain for a very long time, until the Lord Jesus should bring home a very special company of refugees from the planet Earth to take the place of the angels He had lost. But that's getting ahead of the story.

The controversy was not over. Only its battlefield had changed. This earth had become the theater of conflict, but the target of the enemy's rage—still—was Christ, the Creator, the Son of God.

Our first parents were faithfully warned of the fallen angel's presence in the garden. But they had nothing to fear. Only disobedience could place them in any danger.

We have no record of the days that followed, of the unmarred fellowship between Adam and Eve and their Creator. We don't know how long those happy days continued. They were intended to last forever.

But one day, as Jesus watched from heaven, Eve wandered near the one tree that God had placed off bounds. And when she was near enough, a beautiful creature, sitting in the tree and leisurely eating its fruit, began talking to her. She had no idea that the voice was the voice of the fallen angel against whom she had been warned.

And the creature said something like this: "You're beautiful. You've never heard an animal speak, have you? It's this fruit that gives me the power to speak. And just think! If this fruit can make a dumb animal speak, what would it do for you who already have the gift of speech?"

Jesus watched breathlessly. If only she wouldn't listen. If only she would hurry back to Adam. If only she would not touch the fruit. And the agony of Jesus, as He saw her take the fruit and eat it, can never be described!

And then Adam, terrified at what she had done but not wanting to lose her, followed her in rebellion. The happy days were over. Now came the age of tears. Tears on this planet. Tears in heaven. And tears on other worlds!

The Strategy of Rebellion

The fall of man from his high position was the greatest tragedy this planet has ever known. The Garden of Eden was heaven in miniature—all that the wildest imagination could ever dream.

Yet the instigator of that tragedy has downplayed it, ridiculed it, painted it over, until Eden, in the minds of untold millions, is nothing but a myth, and the fall of man, a joke.

"Eden? Oh yes. Where Eve ate the apple." And then an indulgent smile. For who believes it?

Many who doubt the story have probably never read it, though it is so near the beginning of the Bible they'd have to turn at most a few pages to find it. They would be surprised to learn that "the apple" is not mentioned. And probably it has never crossed their minds that the trouble we are in today all began with an act of deliberate choice on the part of two very real people in a very real garden that could properly be called a paradise.

The instigator of rebellion doesn't want us to think of the fall of man as a fall at all. And if you doubt the success of his propaganda, consider this: Doesn't almost every university in the land teach almost as established fact that man has evolved upward from an all-the-way-down beginning in the hazy past—and never fell at all? There is no place in the reasoning of evolution for the fall of man. And of course, if man never fell, he has no need of a Saviour. He can do very nicely on his own, thank you.

The Eden experience, in some versions of the rebel angel's

propaganda, is freely admitted as fact. But it is praised as man's courageous break with all restriction, his declaration of independence. A triumph, you see, rather than a tragedy.

Whatever the reasoning, the defection of our first parents is usually thought of as something very, very trivial—not worthy of the attention you would give a leaky faucet!

Listen! The game that the fallen angel is playing is certainly a lot *bigger* than we ever dreamed. The conflict between Christ and Satan involves all heaven and earth. And it absorbs the attention of the watching worlds. The stakes in the game are the souls of men. And the universe stands or falls with the outcome.

Too many of us, sincere though we may be, have skimmed too quickly over the account of the fall of man in the third chapter of Genesis. We know that our first parents had been told (Genesis 2:17) that one tree in the garden was off bounds and that death would follow disobedience. In this third chapter Eve approaches the tree, and a serpent talks her into eating the forbidden fruit. That's about all that has registered with a lot of us.

We have been like a little boy watching a parade through a knothole. And it's hard to get the big view. We need to move back to a spot where we can get an unobstructed view of the whole parade. We need to view the broad expanse of this cosmic controversy that involves us so directly. We need to know what is going on, what the issues are. We need to know something of what to expect from the enemy.

What general in active combat would not be delighted to come into possession of a document outlining the strategy of the enemy in detail? But that, I believe, is exactly what we can discover in the third chapter of Genesis. Read it carefully. Give it some time. And you may be surprised at what a find it is. For the fallen angel's strategy in that first encounter on this planet is basically what we can expect of him today. It has changed only in detail.

Notice first that Satan did not want his true identity known. He used a disguise, he used a medium, he used impersonation. And here, right at the beginning, he used the supernatural, he used a psychic phenomenon to attract the attention of his victim. The serpent, in unscarred Eden, was undoubtedly a beautiful creature. But a serpent could not speak. That is what attracted Eve—a serpent talking. We can expect the same use of the supernatural today—in infinite variation.

Satan in the garden, speaking through the serpent, making it a medium, lost no time in planting *doubt* in Eve's mind—doubts about the credibility of God's word. "Has God said you would die if you eat this fruit? Why, God knows better. He knows you won't die. He knows that if you eat this fruit you will be like a god."

Satan goes so far as to directly contradict God's word. God had said, "If you eat the fruit, you will die." And Satan says, "You will *not* die." We can expect him today not to tell the truth. For Jesus said of Satan, "He is a liar, and the father of it." John 8:44, KJV.

The fallen angel also uses half-truths. In fact, the more truth he mingles with his error, the more palatable it is to his victims—and the more dangerous. Notice his implication that God was keeping something back from our first parents—something He didn't want them to know.

That's true—very true. God *didn't* want them to know what it's like to be so haunted with guilt that you can't sleep. He *didn't* want them to know what it's like to die. He *didn't* want them to know what it's like to see a beloved son take the life of his brother. He wanted to keep that knowledge from them and from us!

But Satan called it tyranny. He said God didn't care!

"You are free to eat from any tree in the garden," God had said, "but you must not eat from the tree of the knowledge of good and evil, for when you eat of it you will surely die." Genesis 2:16, 17, NIV.

This was not an arbitrary ultimatum. It was a warning, given in love, of what the sure result of disobedience would be. Death does not follow disobedience because a threat has been made. It follows because that's just the way it works. The apostle Paul said it this way: "The wages of sin is death." Romans 6:23, KJV.

Satan, in the days when he was still the son of the morning, knew that the wages of sin is death. He had been faithfully warned of where his steps were leading. But he refused to turn back. And now, banished from heaven, past the point of no return, he knew that one day he must die. And as he saw the beautiful earth that the Son of God had made and the happy couple created to rule over it, his fury knew no bounds. He determined to destroy both *it* and *them*. He vowed that, if he must die, he would take the human race with him.

How did he propose to accomplish this? An important part of Satan's strategy would be to convince men that they *would not* and *could not* die—that God had made them with an immortal soul, making death impossible. They could live as they pleased. Nothing would happen. They could laugh at God's warnings.

But God was guilty of no such mistake. He was far too wise to build immortality into men and women before they had demonstrated that they could be trusted with never-ending life!

Another key element in the enemy's strategy surfaces in these words, "For God knows that when you eat of it your eyes will be opened, and you will be like God, knowing good and evil." Genesis 3:5, NIV.

"You will be like God." The strategy hasn't changed at all. We are bombarded with it today. Discover yourself, we are told. Know yourself. There's a spark of divinity within you—just bring it out. You're a little god yourself. The line has a thousand variations. And it all means this: Go it alone. Be independent. You don't need God.

That's the way the controversy on this planet began. At issue here, as it had been in heaven, was the authority of God—His throne, His law, and His character. The chief target of the enemy's wrath—the Son of God, His position, His creatorship. The goal of rebellion now and here—control of the minds of men. Their worship—whether by choice or by force. And their destruction.

Do you understand a little better now the tragedy of Eden? Satan had won the first round of the contest. He had persuaded our first parents to sell themselves into a slavery that, without divine intervention, could never be broken.

What would God do now?

Sometimes You Need a Prophet

In many living things there is some instrument of guidance. The birds travel thousands of miles and yet return to the same place. The bat, blindfolded, can fly between iron bars without touching them. And they say it is impossible to lose a homing pigeon.

Has man alone been set adrift without some inner compass? Is that why millions turn to the daily horoscope for guidance? Or to the fortune teller? To those who read the palm, the tea leaf, the crystal ball?

Is that why we are so quick to follow a leader—even if the leader cannot see where he is going?

Some of you may be familiar with the writings of Bruce Barton. But you may not be acquainted with the writings of his father, William B. Barton. Here is a gem—just as he wrote it:

"We sojourned in Egypt, I and Keturah, and we rode on donkeys, and also on camels. Now of all the beasts that ever were made, the camel is the most ungainly and preposterous, and also the most picturesque. And he taketh himself very seriously.

"And we beheld a string of five camels that belonged in one caravan, and they were tethered every one to the camel in front of him. But the foremost of the camels had on a halter that was tied to the saddle of a donkey. And I spake unto the man of Arabia who had the camels, and inquired of him how he managed it.

"And he said, 'Each camel followeth the one in front and

33

asketh no questions, and I come after and prod up the last camel.' And I said, 'Doth not the first camel consider that there is no other in front of him, but only [a donkey]?'

"And he answered, 'Nay, for the first camel is blind, and knoweth only that there is a pull at his halter. And every other camel followeth as he is led, and I prod up the hindermost one.' And I inquired about the donkey.

"And he said, 'The donkey is too stupid to do anything but keep straight on, and he hath been often over the road.'

"And I said unto Keturah, 'Behold a picture of human life, for on this fashion have the processions of the ages largely been formed. For there be few men who ask otherwise than how the next in front is going, and they blindly follow, each in the track of those who have gone before.'

"And Keturah said, 'But how about the leader?' And I said, 'That is the most profoundest secret of history. For often he who seemed to be the leader was really behind the whole procession.' "

Is any comment needed? It's easy to follow a magnetic personality, one who speaks smooth things and makes us feel good about ourselves. But that smooth-talking leader may be as blind as that lead camel. And the donkey may be headed straight for the ditch—or, perhaps, even for Jonestown!

What we need is a real, genuine prophet. A prophet, you know, is sometimes called a seer—one who can see. A prophet is delegated by God to be the eyes of His people. It was Solomon, the wise man, who said, "Where there is no vision, the people perish." Proverbs 29:18, KJV.

And listen to this: "Have faith in the Lord your God and you will be upheld; have faith in his prophets and you will be successful." 2 Chronicles 20:20, NIV.

Have faith in His prophets. It just isn't safe to go blindly along, following our noses, carving out a path that seems right to us. For "there is a way that seems right to a man, but in the end it leads to death." Proverbs 14:12, NIV.

Ancient Babylon didn't need a prophet—certainly not one who spoke for the God of the Hebrews. Were not the gods of Babylon superior to all other gods? Was not this great Babylon, ruler of the world, the kingdom that would endure forever? So Babylon thought and planned.

But Babylon *would* need a prophet—and soon. It would need a prophet desperately. The king would have some strange dreams—and not a one of his boasting counselors would be able to make sense out of them. A hand would one day write in letters of fire upon the palace wall. And none but a prophet of God would be able to read the fiery words.

A thousand miles away from the proud city, a teenager was growing straight and tall, never dreaming what God had in mind for him.

I wonder what he was like. I wonder if his father helped him fly kites in the March wind. And I wonder if his father taught him a truth that Will Carleton would one day put in rhyme: "Boys flying kites haul in their white-winged birds;/You can't do that way when you're flying words." Surely his father must have taught him that a man's destiny may depend upon his ability to say No.

His mother must have told him, more than once, the story of Joseph—the boy who was sold into slavery by his jealous brothers. She must have told him how Joseph, far from home, in a strange land where no one knew him, still refused to sin against his God.

Yes, the boy must have had wonderful parents. And he must have seen and shared their sadness as neighbors and friends turned from their loyalty to God and began to worship the senseless gods of the heathen.

And then, one day when he was about eighteen, it suddenly happened. He, like Joseph, was taken captive to a strange land. The king of Babylon had laid seige to Jerusalem. And to show his power and his special disdain for the God of Israel, he took some of the sacred vessels from the temple. And he took captive some of the finest youth, young men of royal line, secretly delighting in the thought that he would soon have them worshiping the gods of Babylon.

Yes, his name was Daniel. And he was being forced to march, with the Chaldean army, the thousand miles to Babylon.

But the king was to be disappointed in some of his plans. For, by the time the army came in sight of the ruins of the tower of Babel Daniel and three of his friends had determined not to compromise. They would be true to their God, come what may!

The first test was not long in coming. King Nebuchadnezzar determined to prepare the finest of the Hebrew captives to serve in his court. They were to have the very best education. And as a special favor to them, they were to have the same food that was prepared for the king's table.

Wonderful, you say. But there was a problem. Some of the food and wine prepared for the king had been offered to Babylon's idols, and eating that food would have been considered an act of communion with these false gods. Daniel and his friends couldn't do that without denying the God of heaven.

And there was another problem. These fine young men had been taught that a simple, nonstimulating diet would give them clearer minds and better health. And certainly, if they wished to stand against the temptations of this wicked city, they would need clear minds.

True, it seemed a little thing, even inconsequential. Wasn't it more important, right at the beginning, not to offend the king by refusing his favors? But Daniel and his friends recognized what was involved. Daniel, acting as spokesman, tactfully asked, and was granted, permission to eat the simple food to which they were accustomed. And they came through with flying colors. You can read the story in the first chapter of Daniel's book.

So began their education in a strange land. And while they were learning the Chaldean language and preparing for positions in Babylon's court, God was preparing Daniel to be His prophet.

Why did God need a prophet in the court of Babylon, that great center of pagan worship? What did He have in mind?

First of all, God loved Babylon, just as He loves every wicked city. He loved its proud king.

You see, God had intended for Israel to be a light to the surrounding nations. But Israel had failed miserably. Israel itself had gone tramping after forbidden gods.

God wanted Babylon to know what He was like. He wanted

the pagan capital to see that He was not like the heathen gods who had to be bribed and appeased. Rather, He was a God of love. He was aware of everything that happens to His children. He was a God willing to come down personally to deliver them, or walk with them through the fire.

The book of Daniel is a fascinating book. It is full of deliverances. It tells how God delivered Daniel from hungry lions, and his friends from an overheated furnace. It tells how Jesus would come to deliver His people from their sins. And it tells of a time, still future, when God's people will be delivered from the worst time of trouble this world has ever known.

Do you begin to see why you personally need to understand the book of Daniel? Could anything better prepare you for the crisis that soon we must all face?

Tell me. Would you have the courage to stand alone as did Daniel and his friends—risk the displeasure of the king and even their lives?

And then another question. If God wanted to prepare you to stand in a crisis, how do you think He would go about it?

You say, "I suppose He would give me some little tests along the way."

And you are exactly right!

You see, it's the little tests along the way that determine how we will do in the big crisis. For if we always take the easy way out—the popular way, perhaps—in everyday decisions, we will do the same thing in a crisis. We will have formed the habit. And we are not likely to change it then.

If Daniel and his friends had failed that first test, what would have happened? We probably would never have heard of a prophet Daniel—or of his deliverance from hungry lions. Nor would we have heard of his three friends and how the Son of God walked with them in the flames of the fiery furnace.

This world—and Babylon—and you and I—would have lost much if they had failed that first test. We are richer—and God is richer—because four young men had the courage to say No! Sometimes there is no better way to score points for God in this controversy that involves us all!

The Confounding of the Psychics

It is reported that the Ford Motor Company asked Charles A. Jayne, author of a horoscope column in the *New York Daily News*, to chart the future of the new Mustang automobile. Jayne responded with this horoscope:

"Those born September 21 [the date the Mustang was introduced] are particularly endowed with the basic qualities of efficiency and resourcefulness. Your moon in relation to Uranus indicates you are highly innovative and highly individualistic. Essentially, your planetary pattern is so well-balanced that you should be assured of a productive and successful life."

Just a public relations gimmick? Yes. But thousands of buyers took it seriously and bought Mustangs because of it.

Who made the horoscope come true? The stars? Or the buyers?

It was in the pagan superstition of Mesopotamia, land of the twin rivers, the Euphrates and the Tigris, that astrology was born. Some think it originated in that area as early as three thousand years ago. At any rate, Babylon soon became the center for the practice of this divining art. And Nebuchadnezzar, most powerful of the Babylonian kings, made no secret of the fact that he had an assortment of astrologers and other psychics in his court.

How did God feel about these psychics and their pagan superstitions? How did He feel about their various forecasting tools? This is not hard to discover, for He specifically prohibited their use among His people. His words are a devastating condemna-

39

tion of the occult. Listen: "Thou shalt not learn to do after the abominations of those nations. There shall not be found among you any one that . . . useth divination [fortune-telling], or an observer of times [astrologer], or an enchanter [magician], or a witch, or a charmer, or a consulter with familiar spirits [a medium who uses a spirit guide], or a wizard [clairvoyant, clairaudient, or psychic seer], or a necromancer [medium who consults the so-called spirits of the dead]. For all that do these things are an abomination unto the Lord." Deuteronomy 18:9-12, KJV.

Abomination. I guess you know what that word means!

Why was God so hard on the psychics? Because a practitioner of the occult was openly giving allegiance to God's enemy, the fallen angel. It's as simple as that.

Is it that God doesn't want us to know anything about the future? Is He trying to keep us in the dark? No, not at all. We read from the prophet Amos, "Surely the Lord God will do nothing, but he revealeth his secret unto his servants the prophets." Amos 3:7, KJV.

Unto His servants the psychics? No. His servants the prophets. And how does He communicate with the prophets? "If there be a prophet among you, I the Lord will make myself known unto him in a vision, and will speak unto him in a dream." Numbers 12:6, KJV.

Visions and dreams. Not through mediums. Not through spirit guides. Not through crystal balls. Not through horoscope charts. Visions and dreams!

God wants us to know about the future. But He wants us to get it straight.

But back to Babylon. God saw that mighty empire, steeped in the occult. From the king on down they worshipped other gods and turned to the psychics for counsel.

Did God say, "Babylon is wicked. Babylon is without hope. Let her go!"?

No. God loved Babylon. He wouldn't let her go without doing everything He could to win her. And he determined to go right to the top of that powerful empire. He would put a prophet right into the court of that proud and arrogant king. And that prophet would be a young Hebrew captive—Daniel.

God wanted the attention of the proud king. And He was about to challenge the claims of the psychics. He began by giving Nebuchadnezzar a dream—and then causing him to forget it. The king was sure of only one thing—that the forgotten dream was something very important.

Now the psychics were in trouble—more trouble than they realized. Interpreting a dream was no problem. Anybody could do that. Anybody could concoct some sort of interpretation—if they knew what the dream was. But, in their estimation, this king was being ridiculously unreasonable: he was demanding that they tell him what he had dreamed—*or die!*

The psychics panicked. What if this was a trick? What if the king hadn't really forgotten the dream? What if he was just testing them? They didn't dare make up a dream. They complained, "It's too hard. Nobody asks anything like that of a psychic!"

But the king was unrelenting. He was determined to find out what he had dreamed. And when they couldn't tell him, he condemned them all to death. And because the king didn't know the difference between a prophet and a psychic, Daniel was rounded up with the others to be executed.

The king didn't know the difference between a prophet and a psychic. But God proposed to show him!

Daniel now fearlessly took his life in his hands and asked to appear before the king. But first he asked for time to pray to his God, promising to give the king both the dream and its interpretation. The king was so impressed by Daniel's quiet confidence—and so anxious to know what he had dreamed—that he granted Daniel's request.

And did God fail His young servant? No. Never! In a night vision He revealed to him both the dream and its meaning.

So it was that the next morning Daniel stood before the king, who had been anxiously waiting for him. Was it possible that this unassuming young captive could do what his once-trusted psychic counselors could not? "Can you tell me the dream?" he asked.

Yes, he could. And he did. Follow along with the story, if you will, in the second chapter of Daniel's book, beginning with verse 31. Daniel told the king that in his dream he had seen a tall, magnificent statue. That was it! The king leaned forward, unable to hide his excitement. That was exactly what he had seen. It all came back to him now. He listened breathlessly as Daniel described the statue.

Its head, said the prophet, was gold, its chest and arms were silver, its thighs bronze, its legs iron, and its feet—part iron and part clay.

The king sat there amazed. It checked perfectly with what he had seen. But something had happened to the statue. Would Daniel know that too?

Yes! A huge boulder had struck the statue on its feet. And the entire statue was ground to powder and blown away like chaff.

Daniel hadn't missed a thing. And now he continued with the meaning of the dream. "You," he said simply, "are the head of gold."

The proud king liked that! It seemed very appropriate that he should be the golden head. Evidently Daniel's God was aware of his greatness and his power!

But of course the king has been flattered before. Could it be, he wondered, that Daniel was only a clever young politician playing for royal favor? No, Daniel's next words settled that. He declared what no aspiring politician would ever say: "And after you there will arise another kingdom inferior to you." Verse 39, NASB.

The king *didn't* like that! That was enough to spoil any monarch's ambitious dreams. Daniel's God was not telling the king what he wanted to be told. Daniel's God was telling him that his kingdom would *not* last forever. It would be succeeded by another—and an inferior one at that!

Is it any wonder that at a later time, with Daniel's words still rankling in his mind, the king had a great statue constructed *all* of gold—the way he was determined it would be? He had it set upon the plain of Dura and commanded everybody to worship it or burn!

But Daniel continued: There would be a third kingdom, represented by the bronze, and then a fourth world kingdom, strong as iron.

What was God revealing to the king? Was He telling him that there would soon be an assassination in his court? Was He telling him not to get into his carriage the next day because the "stars" wouldn't be right?

No, friend! No! God was revealing to that ancient king—and to you and me—the mighty sweep of history in advance!

And did it happen that way? Yes, God's prophets have never been wrong—not even once. History has followed this prophecy of Daniel as it has followed every other Bible prophecy—like a blueprint!

Babylon was conquered by Cyrus the Persian even in Daniel's day. It happened during the feast of Belshazzar. Remember the writing on the wall?

The Medes and the Persians, represented by the two silver arms of the statue, ruled for about two hundred years. Then came Alexander the Great and the bronze kingdom, followed by the iron kingdom, the fourth, which has to be Rome. It could be no other!

Four successive kingdoms. Wouldn't you think there would be a fifth? But no. Never again would this massive land area come under the rule of one man. Rome was the last of such empires!

Daniel went on to explain that the iron kingdom would be divided. It would break up into ten kingdoms, represented by the ten toes of the statue. (See Daniel 7:24.) And those ten kingdoms, the modern nations of Europe, would never again be reunited permanently under the rule of one man. Listen to this: "And in that you saw the iron mixed with common clay, they will combine with one another in the seed of men; but they will not adhere to one another, even as iron does not combine with pottery." Verse 43, NASB.

What do you think of that? They will not adhere to one another. The nations of Europe will not stick together! How could God have said it better?

"They will not adhere to one another." Those seven words have collided head on with the dreams of every would-be dictator since the Caesars. They are the reason for history's uncanny repetition as one man after another, aspiring to rule the world, has gone down in defeat!

But Daniel was not through. "And in the days of those kings the God of heaven will set up a kingdom which will never be destroyed, and that kingdom will not be left for another people; it will crush and put an end to all these kingdoms, but it will itself endure forever." Verse 44, NASB.

In the days of those kings—the nations of modern Europe—as the next great event in earth's history, God will intervene. The Lord Jesus will appear in the skies. And His kingdom will never end!

Is it any wonder that Nebuchadnezzar was profoundly impressed? God had just demonstrated—for him and for us—the wide and striking contrast between the trivial fortune-telling of the psychics and the stately march of divine prediction. And the psychics were confounded! God had outlined the future as no man or woman could ever do.

Friend, I wonder if you realize what a risk Daniel took when he made this prediction—if God was not speaking through him. I wonder if you realize how unlikely every part of Daniel's prophecy was—by human standards. His was no lucky guess. Who could have guessed, when Babylon was at the height of its glory, that it was soon to fall, and to a lesser power? Who could have guessed that four world kingdoms would not be followed by a fifth, that there would be four and no more, and that the fourth would be divided into ten and never get together again?

Who can possibly explain why, with all our sophisticated weapons, with all our burst of technology, no nation of modern times has been able to form a world empire—when Nebuchadnezzar, Cyrus, Alexander and the Caesars, with their inferior weaponry, could do it? Yet one aspiring dictator after another since the last of the four empires has bumped his head against Daniel's prophecy. And it has refused to budge!

What chance was there, if Daniel spoke only in his own wisdom, that every point in his prophecy—a prophecy covering the sweep of centuries, even millenniums—would be fulfilled? Maybe one chance in seventy-five million? I don't know.

Daniel, like other Old Testament prophets, walked far, far

out on a limb. But he took no risk at all. For it was God who was speaking.

How wonderful it is that God has chosen to reveal the future to His children! How reassuring it is to know what the future holds, to know that God is in control, to know that not one of His words will fail!

The books of Daniel and the Revelation, we shall discover, are closely tied together. Both were written especially for our day. Both draw back the curtain of the future.

But these books were intended to do more than give us a peek at history's last chapter. They were meant not merely to reveal the future, but to prepare us for it.

Why is it that the first half of Daniel's book consists almost entirely of stories? The first test that confronted Daniel and his friends when they arrived in Babylon—the matter of the king's food. The experience of Daniel—when he was thrown into a den of hungry lions—because he prayed to his God. The experience of Daniel's three friends on the plain of Dura—when they were commanded to worship the statue that the proud king had constructed.

Entertaining? Yes, definitely. But that isn't why those experiences are there. The book of Revelation, in the thirteenth chapter, makes it clear that tests equally severe await *us*. In the near future we shall have to make some life-or-death choices. And God wants us to know that He will be with us— just as He was with Daniel and his friends. For once again, as in the days of Daniel, the music will sound, and the band will play, as on the plain of Dura. And almost everybody will bow down—to a counterfeit Christ. It will take God-given courage to stand tall and straight and wait for the real Jesus!

Decoding Bible Prophecy

The Kennedy twins—Ginny and Gracie—were a mystery. They seemed happy enough. But they baffled everyone. Their hyperspeed chatter sounded "as if a tape recorder were turned on fast forward with an occasional understandable word jumping out."

The problem was that at six years old they still couldn't speak English. For a while, some thought they were retarded. But they were far too bright for mentally retarded classes. Apparently they had developed a language of their own, with a vocabulary of hundreds of exotic words along with strange half-English and half-German phrases.

Ginny and Gracie were soon among the world's most celebrated twins. Language experts tried to figure them out. Finally speech pathologists learned their private language. But when they tried to use it, the girls seemed not to understand. They just laughed.

Some feel the books of Daniel and Revelation, the two books written especially for our day, have a secret language of their own, that they are talking to each other in completely incomprehensible phrases. Some say that we aren't supposed to understand these books—that they are sealed books. But wouldn't it be strange if God should take the two books especially targeted to our day, filled with vital information essential to our survival, and lock them away from us in a code He knew we could never break? Is that the kind of God He is? Hardly!

The truth is that a portion of the book of Daniel *was* sealed

(Daniel 12:4), but only until "the time of the end." It isn't sealed anymore, for we now live in the time of the end. And the book of Revelation never was sealed (Revelation 22:10). The very word *revelation* means "something revealed." In the first chapter (Revelation 1:3) a blessing is pronounced upon those who read and act upon what is written in the book. And in the final chapter (Revelation 22:18, 19) a fearful warning is given to anyone who would presume to either add or subtract from this prophetic book. Evidently God intends for us to understand the messages He gives us.

But you say, "I've tried. But I can't make any sense out of all those animals and horns and trumpets and everything."

I know. The human mind is noted for its gullibility. And yet our capacity for belief does have limitations. It is a little difficult to believe that a single wild animal could devour the whole earth. Or that the littlest horn on the head of a goat could cast stars to the ground and stamp on them. We would have trouble believing that a modest number of twenty-four-hour days could span centuries, even millenniums.

So when we encounter such statements in Bible prediction we can only conclude that the wild animals and the horns and those particular twenty-four-hour days were never intended to be taken literally. Rather, we are dealing with prophetic symbols.

But someone says, "But how can we ever figure them out? And why doesn't God just say what He means, if He wants us to understand?"

Millions have felt that way. Pictures, of course, can say a lot. Our newspapers often use cartoons to put a point across. And if God uses animals to represent nations, don't we sometimes do the same thing? The American eagle? The Russian bear?

But you are right. Plain words are clearest of all. So why doesn't God come right out and say what He means? Is he trying to make it hard for us? Is that it?

No, not at all. God wants us to understand. It is imperative that we do. And wherever God in the scriptures is telling us how men are saved—the essentials of salvation—He speaks in language we have no difficulty understanding. The gospel is not given in symbols. Illustrations, yes. Parables, yes. Jesus often put truth into a story, so that His enemies would listen all the way through before they realized the story had to do with them.

But when God through His prophets was revealing history in advance, when He was outlining the future of His children, it was often necessary to trace the future activities of nations unfriendly to Him and His people. To name names would be to invite the destruction of the book by its enemies. So the answer is simple. God used symbols in order to protect the Book and His people from its enemies and theirs.

But how can we figure out these symbols? How can we know what they mean?

First of all, in some cases there is no figuring out to be done. In some cases the Bible tells us what they mean. You recall that when Daniel told Nebuchadnezzar what he had dreamed, the prophet immediately interpreted its meaning.

In the seventh chapter of Daniel, the prophet is shown a vision involving four beasts and some horns. But in the latter part of the chapter he is told that the beasts are kings, or kingdoms (verse 17), and that the ten horns are ten kings (verse 24).

So we have learned one symbol. A beast represents a kingdom, a nation. The nation may be good or bad. The Bible does not use the term *beast* in a derogatory way.

Daniel is given another vision in chapter 8, and later the angel Gabriel himself comes back to explain its symbols (verse 16).

Another symbol. In prophecy a woman is used to represent a church—a lovely and beautiful woman represents God's true church (Jeremiah 6:2 and Revelation 12:1-5) and a corrupt woman represents a false church, a fallen church (Revelation 17:3-5).

Notice that the symbols are not random, meaning one thing on one occasion and later something else. The symbols are consistent, whether we are studying Daniel or the Revelation, the Old Testament or the New.

We are not left to concoct our own meaning of the symbols. They are defined for us in Scripture—so far as we need to know them. It may take a little searching. It may take much searching. But they are there.

The trouble is that some people do not bother to search. They seem to enjoy dreaming up answers out of whole cloth, with little or no Bible support for their speculations. At the present time, there is terrific interest in Bible prophecy—even among those who know very little of Scripture. Everybody wants to know what is going to happen, and sometimes it seems as if everybody has his own interpretation of what he reads. But Bible prophecy is not a toy for the speculators, to be manipulated to suit one's liking. It is the expression of the infallible wisdom of God. And when last-day prophecy happens—when Bible prediction is fulfilled, it will happen only one way, not a thousand ways. It will happen as God predicted it will happen—without any reference whatever to how "it seems to me."

One of the greatest pitfalls we face in interpreting Bible prophecy is trying to make a scripture passage symbolic when it is really literal.

But how can we tell which is which? The best rule is to consider everything in Scripture as literal unless there is good reason to believe it is symbolic. Read the context carefully. Many interpretations today are nothing more than personal preferences. "This is the way I would like it to be," as one person put it.

It's so easy to label as symbolic anything we do not like. But when the Bible speaks of the worst earthquake this planet has ever known (Revelation 16:18), it means exactly what it says. And when it predicts hailstones the weight of a talent (Revelation 16:21), it isn't talking about frosted balloons.

I am not talking here about something trivial. We are really in trouble when we begin writing off as symbol or myth or legend whatever we don't like in the Word of God.

Here's what can happen. Millions of people, reading the first chapters of Genesis, have written them off as myth or legend. Then they read a little farther and find it hard to believe that a global flood ever happened. After all, they've never seen one. So they write that off too. Then, at some point, they encounter the books of Daniel and Revelation. And along with the good news

those books contain, there are serious warnings about God's final judgments, His final accounting with men. But if they have
symbolized away the beginning of this planet, they will likely
do the same with its end. They will file away the coming judgment by fire along with the judgment by water in Noah's day,
and forget them both. God says they are "willingly ignorant."
See 2 Peter 3:5-7, KJV. And that ignorance can be fatal.

In other words, it is a *mistake* to call things literal when they
are only symbolic. But it is *absolutely fatal* to call something
symbolic, such as the judgment, and find out too late that it is
very, very real!

We might call this way of thinking the "symbolic escape."
But the attempt to escape reality by symbolizing it, by juggling
Scripture, reinterpreting it, twisting it, misapplying it, maneu-
vering it, shoving it out of where it belongs and wedging it into
where it doesn't—this refuge of wishful thinking, this house
constructed of self-made symbols, will collapse like water in the
final crisis!

Another caution. It is wise to tread softly with unfulfilled
prophecy, wise not to read into a prophecy details which are not
there. Many a sincere expositor of divine prediction has embar-
rassed himself by being too dogmatic about *exactly how* a
prophecy is going to be fulfilled. There is always the temptation
to go farther than the prophecy goes, to explain what the
prophet has not explained.

Jesus once said to His disciples, "I have told you now before it
happens, so that when it does happen you will believe." John
14:29, NIV.

It is usually *fulfilled* prophecy that makes believers. It was
after His crucifixion that the disciples of Jesus boldly pointed
out how He had fulfilled Old Testament prophecy. It was *after*
His crucifixion, after His resurrection, that Jesus, walking
with two of His followers on the way to Emmaus, "beginning at
Moses and all the prophets . . . expounded unto them in all the
scriptures the things concerning himself." Luke 24:27, KJV.

Bible prophecy holds a special fascination for this generation—that probably because nearly everyone senses that we
are approaching some kind of crisis. Time prophecies are espe-

cially intriguing. And frequently there is someone who can't resist the temptation to set a time for the end of the world—supposedly backed up by Scripture.

This is unfortunate, for predictions that fail lead to embarrassment and discouragement. For those looking on, seeing one prediction after another fail and not knowing that such predictions have had no foundation in Scripture, may decide that they want nothing to do with any Bible prophecies. And that, of course, delights the fallen angel.

Actually there is no need to take seriously any prediction that sets a definite time for our Lord's return and for the end of this world as we know it. Jesus said plainly, "No one knows, however, when that day and hour will come—neither the angels in heaven, nor the Son; the Father alone knows." Matthew 24:36, TEV.

There are, however, time prophecies in the Bible. They do not reach to the end of the world, but they are extremely important. Much depends on them, and it is urgent that we understand prophetic calculation.

Both Daniel and Revelation foretell a time of persecution of God's people. So important is this time period that it is mentioned seven times. In Daniel 7:25, KJV, it is expressed as lasting for "a time and times and the dividing of time." In Daniel 12:7, KJV, we read that "it shall be for a time, times, and an half." In Revelation 12:6, KJV, the same time period is said to be "a thousand two hundred and threescore days." In verse 14 it is "a time, and times, and half a time." And in chapter 13, verse 5, it is said to continue for "forty and two months." See also Revelation 11:2, 3.

Is this confusing? That is understandable. But the confusion lifts when we discover that in Bible prophecy a day is often used to represent a literal year. This is a principle recognized by most Bible expositors.

Using this principle, the "thousand two hundred and three score days" become 1260 years. Forty-two months of thirty days each are also 1260 days, or literal years. The Aramaic word translated "time" or "times" is used several times in the fourth chapter of Daniel, where "seven times" obviously means "seven years." Scholars generally agree that in Daniel 7:25 the translation should be "two times" rather than simply a plural. And the word translated "dividing" may also be translated "half." So the Revised Standard Version, which reads "a time, two times, and half a time," is clearer and in this case more correct than some other translations. A year, two years, and half a year equal once again 1260 prophetic days, or literal years.

But you say, "All months are not thirty days in length, and our year contains 365 days, not 360."

True. Actually our year is 365.2422 days in length, and we adjust with leap years. But God kept time prophecies simple and thus easy to understand. In prophetic calculation a month has thirty days, a year 360 days.

In other words, a prophetic day stands for a *solar* year. And a prophetic year, or "time" (made up of 360 prophetic days), stands for 360 literal, natural, solar years.

This year-day principle was not new, even in Daniel's day. You recall that Jacob served his uncle seven years for Rachel, whom he loved, only to be tricked into marrying Leah. He then agreed to "fulfil her week" (Genesis 29:27, KJV) and served seven more years for Rachel. A week—seven years.

When the Hebrews, on their way from Egypt, came up to the Jordan River, they spent forty days spying out the land on the other side and concluded they couldn't handle its giants. Because of their lack of faith in God they were sentenced to wander in the wilderness forty years (Numbers 14:34)—a year for each day spent in spying out the land.

Ezekiel was instructed to illustrate his prophecy by lying on his side for forty days (Ezekiel 4:6)—each day for a year.

Our problem, in interpreting a Bible prediction involving time, is to discover whether the time period is literal or prophetic. Some contend that the 1260 days are literal days, not years. But a prophecy definitely set in the Christian era, such as Revelation 12:6, cannot be pushed back into Old Testament times. Was Jesus, who was the real Author of the Revelation (see chapter 1, verse 1), unaware that this prophecy had already been fulfilled?

If taking a time period to be literal doesn't make sense, when it leads us to absurd conclusions, we can know we are on the wrong track. For when we get it right, it will fit into history with a precision that leaves no room for doubt. Prophecy, said the apostle Peter, is like a light that shines along the course of history, illuminating the future before it happens. 2 Peter 1:19.

So much for the mechanics of decoding prophetic time. We will deal later with the fulfillment of the 1260-year prediction. And at the appropriate time we will probe Daniel's prophecy of 2300 years (Daniel 8:14), which includes mathematical proof that Jesus was who He claimed to be. It is the longest period of prophetic time in the Bible, reaching farther toward our day than any other time prophecy—to the year 1844. Divine prophecy yields no specific date beyond it. And what really happened in 1844 has staggering significance for every rider of this planet, including you and me!

But first, what was happening behind the scenes during these long, dull years of the prophets? Why didn't Jesus come to earth sooner? And what of the fallen angel? Were his malignant attacks against Jesus in a period of remission?

The Year 2000

Come with me to the year 2000. It's not so far away, you know. What will life be like in the twenty-first century?

Picture the place where you will work. Imagine the futuristic vehicle you will own—maybe your personal space shuttle! And fancy the exotic new food to tempt your taste buds. Will there be enough to feed us all?

Will our cities be centers of commerce and culture—or playgrounds of rats and gangs? Will we enjoy peace on earth—or suffer the horrors of doomsday?

We are brimming with curiosity about the future. But, even more, we crave security. We *need* to know what's ahead for us and our loved ones. And we *can* know more than you may think.

Will Jesus return to earth by the year 2000? Many believe He will. Others wonder whether nuclear war will erase the human race first. How can we know what's waiting around the corner? Who can we trust to guide us into the future?

Whenever my wife Nellie and I shop for groceries, we see the colorful tabloids at the checkout counters. You've seen them too. Sometimes the supermarket psychics offer us bold, new predictions. Often they simply recycle the same headlines from the year before. Many disappointed readers have learned not to put faith in their forecasts.

We get more trustworthy information from God in the Bible. Knowing the end from the beginning, our heavenly Father has unfolded our future in the prophecies of Revelation. This last of

56   AMAZING PROPHECIES

Scripture's sixty-six books was recorded about 96 A.D. by the apostle John while exiled on the remote island of Patmos. It's full of exciting and essential information for us today.

Would you like to discover God's plan for this planet? Then join me as we explore Revelation's fascinating forecasts. Perhaps you've been avoiding Revelation. Many Christians recoil in fear from its beasts and dragons, hailstorms and earthquakes. But there's no reason to be afraid.

I am reminded of that dark and stormy night long ago when Jesus walked on water. Picture the scene. While gale-force winds roar at the frightened disciples, the raging Sea of Galilee threatens to swallow them alive. Now a ghostlike figure appears. And it's moving toward them! Their fear becomes heart-pounding panic. Just when their doom seems sealed, the floating phantom speaks with the Master's comforting voice: "It is I; be not afraid." The storm is stilled.

What an experience! The object of terror turned out to be a revelation of Jesus, their friend. This is what we find with the book of Revelation. All anxiety vanishes when we read its opening words in chapter 1, verse 1.

"The Revelation of Jesus Christ, which God gave Him to show His servants—things which must shortly take place."

You can now see why we need not fear the book of Revelation. It simply reveals the Lord Jesus Christ and His blueprint for our future. Our time invested in this book will be richly rewarded. Look at verse 3: "Blessed is he who reads and those who hear the words of this prophecy, and keep those things which are written in it; for the time is near."

Would you like to claim these special benefits reserved for you in studying this book? Then let's get started right now. First I'll introduce you to Revelation and explain the secrets of decoding its symbols. Let's read verses 5 and 6: "From Jesus Christ, the faithful witness, the firstborn from the dead, and the ruler over the kings of the earth. To Him who loved us and washed us from our sins in His own blood, and has made us kings and priests to His God and Father, to Him be glory and dominion forever and ever. Amen."

Here we see Jesus presented as our Saviour, risen from His

death for our sins. How comforting to find the blood of Christ right here in this book which is famous for its beasts. This is the same gospel of salvation so near and dear to every Christian— Jesus the Lamb of God.

A number of years ago a lighthouse was being built on the rockbound coast of Wales. With the building nearly completed, legend has it, one of the workmen stumbled and fell back through the scaffolding to the rocks below.

The other workmen, shocked at what had taken place, didn't dare look down for fear of being unnerved by the sight. Heavyhearted, they backed down the ladders, but to their surprise and happy relief, saw their fellow workman lying upon a mound of grass, shaken and shocked. Bruised, to be sure, but not seriously harmed. Beside him lay a dead lamb. A flock of sheep had been wandering by, and a lamb had broken his fall.

A Lamb broke your fall! A Lamb broke mine—the Lamb of God that takes away the sin of the world! This is the revelation of Jesus we find in the last book of the Bible.

However, Jesus offers the lost human race more than salvation from sin and membership in heaven's royal family. He also rules the kings of the earth. Because He pilots this planet, we're not left to the mercy of governments and terrorists. We need not fear their threats or bombs. Bad things will continue to happen to both good and bad alike. We are living in the midst of a controversy—a conflict between Christ and His enemy, Satan. But friend, nothing happens down here without our Lord's permission. As the song goes, "He's got the whole world in His hands" in spite of its potential for trouble. That's welcome news, isn't it?

Revelation also proclaims the Lord Jesus Christ as the soon-coming King of glory. Notice verse 7, still in the first chapter: "Behold, He is coming with clouds, and every eye will see Him, and they also who pierced Him. And all the tribes of the earth will mourn because of Him. Even so, Amen."

The second coming of Jesus is the great climax of all the books of the Bible. Especially Revelation, which explains through its prophecies what's in store for us before Christ's return.

Before we decode the symbols of this book, let's learn a lesson from Pearl Harbor. Who could ever forget that December day when Japanese bombers swooped from the sky and swept us into World War II? America was caught completely by surprise. But it didn't have to happen that way. You see, United States intelligence had cracked the secret Japanese code. Daily we intercepted messages about an ominous and imminent offensive in the Pacific theater. Yet, incredible as it may seem, nothing much was done to prepare Pearl Harbor for the impending attack. America was asleep that fateful Sunday morning.

We had cracked the code. But we didn't heed the warning. What a shame!

But the United States learned its lesson. We finally put to practice information gained from breaking the code. Six months after Pearl Harbor came the dramatic turning-point, the Battle of Midway. From secret intelligence received through decoding, American pilots knew the precise location of the vulnerable Japanese carriers. With that crucial information we reversed the trend of defeat and went on to win the war.

You can see the lesson for us today. Decoding symbols won't prepare us for the battle ahead. Not unless we put into practice what we discover in the decoded message. We could become expert Bible scholars, yet be lost for not applying what we learn about Christ and His truth.

Are you with me? Now let's find out how to decode these symbols of prophecy. First we must realize that personal opinions, however interesting they may be, contribute nothing to our study. Peter the apostle tells us that no Scripture is open to private interpretation. We only confuse ourselves when we bring our own baggage into the study of the Word. How much better to accept what God offers and follow where He leads.

We learn so much from children! A friend of mine has a little boy named Stevie, who loves to go places with him. Anyplace at all, it matters not where, just so long as he can be with Daddy. Whenever Stevie sees his father heading for the door, car keys in hand, he pleads, "May I go with you?" Only after they start on their way does he ask, "Daddy, where are we going?"

Are we willing to trust our heavenly Father and go anywhere

the Bible leads us? Then we're prepared to decode the prophecies of Revelation.

Just how do we mine the treasures of God's Word? By comparing scripture with scripture. One text unlocks the meaning of another. And since all sixty-six books are linked together, we need to search the whole Bible to understand Revelation.

Now shall we go for a test drive? We hear so much about the beasts of Revelation. What does a beast in prophecy mean?

To decode this symbol we'll visit the book of Daniel. We find special help here in Daniel for understanding Revelation. That is because this book is the Old Testament companion of Revelation, sharing many of the same symbols. Let's read chapter 7, verse 23: "Thus He said: 'The fourth beast shall be a fourth kingdom on earth.' "

So beasts represent kingdoms, or nations. We use the same symbolism in our world today. For example, you know that the United States is symbolized by an eagle. England by a lion. Russia is pictured by a bear. And so on.

Do you see how much satisfaction there can be for you in decoding prophecy? It's simply a matter of probing the Bible to find explanations of its symbols. Simple enough, wouldn't you say?

Let's proceed with our study. Maybe you've noticed that most of the beasts—the nations—of Bible prophecy emerge from water. What then could the symbol of water represent? "And he said to me, 'The waters which you saw, where the harlot sits, are peoples, multitudes, nations, and tongues.' " Revelation 17:15.

There you have the answer. Water means people—multitudes of people. Once again a Bible symbol is echoed in our everyday language. You've heard the expression "a sea of faces." Large crowds of people are described as an ocean. So beasts emerging from the sea represent nations arising from an area of crowded population.

With one important exception, the beasts of Revelation come from the sea—that is, they originate among the crowded countries of the Old World. Let's learn about this special nation in the famous "mark of the beast" chapter, Revelation 13. After reading the description of this unique beast in verse 11, we can decode its meaning. "I saw another beast coming up out of the earth, and he had two horns like a lamb and spoke like a dragon."

What nation does this beast represent? Well, let's fit the pieces of the puzzle together. First, the time setting. This new nation is involved with the final mark-of-the-beast struggle immediately before the coming of Christ, so it's obviously a last-day power. A relatively new nation.

Why does this country arise out of the earth rather than the sea? We learned that water represents an area of many people, so earth would symbolize a new territory away from the crowded Old World of Europe and Asia. Just as soil contains some water, but not much, the nation springs up where there are some people—a few scattered natives, perhaps. We have a new country born on a new continent.

This nation differs from already established powers in another way. Instead of wearing crowns on its horns, like other beasts, it has two horns without crowns. So this New World nation without a crown is not a kingdom. There is no royalty to rule by force. We have here a new form of government. Could this New World republic be the United States?

There are some striking indications. Even the description of a beast with horns like a lamb reminds us of the American buffalo. What do these lamblike horns represent? Christ, of course, is referred to as the Lamb. What was His idea of government? "Render to Caesar the things that are Caesar's, and to God the things that are God's." Mark 12:17. This calls for clear distinction between the government and the church.

In the Old World, church and state formed a unit. Sometimes the government controlled the church. Often it was the other way around—the church ran the government. But America is different. The first amendment forbids Congress from interfering with religion, in order to be fair to everyone. In order to be free.

Now notice something else about our New World republic. Revelation 13 describes its power to lead the whole world. The United States is the most influential nation on earth. What a responsibility!

Unfortunately, the Revelation indicates that America will take some unexpected turns in the near future. The lamblike nation reverses its gentle manners and behaves like a dragon. Evidently some unusual and distressing events will soon occur in America.

What is going to happen? We'll decode the future of the United States in the seventh chapter of this series, "Bloodstained Stars and Stripes." Don't miss that vital study.

Whatever may be waiting for us between now and the year 2000, thank God we don't have to worry about it. Our world may seem out of control, but it's not. God controls our destiny. However confusing and discouraging the outlook may be, remember He will protect His children and fulfill His gracious purpose for our planet.

And the same God who guides this world can bring harmony to your life. No problem of yours is too big for Him to handle. He sustains the stars. And nothing that disturbs your peace is too small for Him to notice, for He organized the tiny atom.

Are you struggling to save your marriage? There's hope and help in Jesus. Have finances forsaken you? Are you hounded by pain or guilt or loneliness? Take heart. Our Father in heaven loves you dearly. Jesus can meet your every need.

But the Saviour won't force Himself on you. He patiently waits for you to ask Him into your life. Here's His gracious invitation: Revelation 3:20. "Behold, I stand at the door and knock. If anyone hears My voice and opens the door, I will come in to him and dine with him, and he with Me."

How much the Saviour enjoys this fellowship with us. Just as we cherish the companionship of our loved ones. The story is told of a little girl from the city visiting Grandma's farm. After a wonderful morning riding horses, they enjoyed a picnic lunch by the river. Then they explored the woods behind the farmhouse. Following supper, they cuddled for stories beside the crackling fireplace. All too soon it was time for bed. As Grandma tucked the yawning girl under the covers, a sudden crash of thunder jolted them both.

"Grandma!" cried the child. "I'm scared! Can I sleep with you?"

Of course, Grandma was delighted to carry the little darling to her room in the darkness. As they settled off to sleep, one last question came. "Grandma, is your face turned toward me?" Assured that it was, the little one found rest at last.

Friend, as the thunders of final crisis roll across our land, we need not be afraid. The book of Revelation assures us Jesus is with us. And His face is always turned toward us.

The Day After Doomsday

You've just finished dinner in your favorite restaurant. Relaxed and refreshed, you rise from the table and head for the coat rack. As you button up against the cold, the wail of an air-raid siren sends a shiver up your spine. "That's strange," you wonder. "What an unusual time to test the Civil Defense System."

Stepping outside, you notice police cars racing by, lights flashing. Helicopters are whirling overhead. Men are shouting—women screaming. What in the world could be happening?

This is no test. This is doomsday.

It has already been twenty minutes since hundreds of missiles roared out of their distant silos. This moment, those demons of death are streaking over the Arctic Circle toward our beautiful and spacious skies.

Fifteen minutes more. That's all we've got left. "Oh God!" somebody screams, "what do we do!" Hell from the clear, blue sky. Everything we own and everyone we love vaporized in a flash. Nothing but ruins and ashes left for the day after.

Could it really happen? We don't like to think about it. I'm not trying to frighten anybody—you know me better than that! But everybody seems to wonder whether our world might be wiped out by nuclear war. What do the Scriptures say? Let's find out. We need to get some background information first; then we will spend the rest of our time in Revelation. I think you'll be delighted as we discover what God has in store for His

63

people. "The day of the Lord will come as a thief in the night, in which the heavens will pass away with a great noise, and the elements will melt with fervent heat; both the earth and the works that are in it will be burned up." "Nevertheless we, according to His promise, look for new heavens and a new earth in which righteousness dwells." 2 Peter 3:10, 13, NKJV.

No question about it—doomsday is on the way. A destruction of this earth by fire. Not by nuclear warheads from man, but by the day of the Lord. Is this bad news? Not for God's committed people. The day after will open the door to happiness ever after for God's people.

Unfortunately for unbelievers, this day of the Lord will be an unexpected surprise. Their pursuit of business and pleasure will be shattered by the sudden destruction of this planet. Doomsday will come as unexpectedly as a thief in the night, the Bible says. And this despite a worldwide warning! On September 21, 1938, a hurricane of monstrous proportions struck the East Coast of the United States. William Manchester, writing about it in his book, *The Glory and the Dream,* says that "the great wall of brine struck the beach between Babylon and Patchogue [Long Island, New York] at 2:30 p.m. So mighty was the power of that first storm wave that its impact registered on a seismograph in Sitka, Alaska, while the spray, carried northward at well over a hundred miles an hour, whitened windows in Montpelier, Vermont.

"As the torrential forty-foot wave approached, some Long Islanders jumped into cars and raced inland. No one knows precisely how many lost that race for their lives, but the survivors later estimated that they had to keep the speedometer over 50 mph all the way."

For some reason the meteorologists—who should have known what was coming and should have warned the public—seemed strangely blind to the impending disaster. Either they ignored their instruments or simply couldn't believe what they read. And, of course, if the forecasters were blind, the public was too.

"Among the striking stories which later came to light," says Manchester, "was the experience of a Long Islander who had bought a barometer a few days earlier in a New York store. It arrived in the morning post September 21, and to his annoyance the needle pointed below 29, where the dial read 'Hurricanes and Tornadoes.' He shook it and banged it against the wall; the needle wouldn't budge. Indignant, he repacked it, drove to the post office, and mailed it back. While he was gone, his house blew away."

That's the way we are. If we can't cope with the forecast, we blame the barometer. Or ignore it. Or throw it away!

Only once in history has a worldwide storm warning been issued. The forecaster was Noah. God Himself had told him to warn the world of a global flood. And Noah showed his own faith in the forecast by beginning at once to build a huge ship in which all who believed the warning could escape.

But human nature was exactly what it is now. The people laughed at Noah, called him a fanatic, a man deranged, made his boat a tourist attraction—and were caught by surprise! History will repeat in our day as we near the end of the world.

Since Christ will come unexpectedly, does that mean the world will be without warning? Not according to the apostle Paul.

Remember Pearl Harbor? The Japanese surprised us even though we had advance warning of their attack. But when those bombers swept down from the sky, we certainly knew they had arrived.

That's how it will be at the return of Jesus. Despite worldwide warnings, the unsaved will be surprised. But the Bible says every eye will see Christ coming. See Revelation 1:7. Every living soul on earth will be watching. Let's read Paul's description of Christ's return in 1 Thessalonians 4:16, 17, "For the Lord Himself will descend from heaven with a shout, with the voice of the archangel, and with the trumpet of God. And the dead in Christ will rise first. Then we who are alive and remain shall be caught up together with them in the clouds to meet the Lord in the air. And thus we shall always be with the Lord." Imagine what it will be like to hear Jesus shout for joy as He descends from heaven. And to hear the mighty trumpet of God. Christ's coming will be the most vocal, the most spectacular event of all time. And not a soul will miss it!

Picture the glorious scene if you can. The Son of God piercing the vaulted heavens, moving down the star-studded highway of the skies, attended by myriads of angels. Then He calls out with a voice of thunder, "Awake, you that sleep in the dust of the earth! Arise to everlasting life!"

And loved ones you have lost will hear. That voice calling the dead will be heard the world around. Families will be united. Children snatched away by death will be placed again in their mothers' arms. What a reunion day!

As the resurrected saints are drawn upward to meet Jesus, we who are alive join them in the air. Imagine the feeling! Defying gravity, we soar through the sky. Without a spacesuit, we sail past the stars up to our heavenly home. What a reunion day! What a homecoming we'll enjoy when Jesus comes! What awaits us when we pass through heaven's pearly gates? Let's read our Lord's familiar promise. You probably know it by heart.

"Let not your heart be troubled; you believe in God, believe also in Me. In My Father's house are many mansions; if it were not so, I would have told you. I go to prepare a place for you. And if I go and prepare a place for you, I will come again and receive you unto Myself; that where I am, there you may be also." John 14:1-3.

And what a welcome that will be! Angels crowding about us, singing songs of joyous praise! A homecoming banquet to surpass any dinner we've ever enjoyed on earth! And, best of all, the Father Himself will introduce us to our paradise home.

And what a home it will be—heavenly mansions! What will they be like? Certainly more glorious than the richest dwellings on earth. Even more breathtaking than Hearst Castle!

Come with me up the beautiful California coast to the village of San Simeon. Set back from the beach in the hills lies the most magnificent building in North America. It is the secluded castle built in the 1920s by the famed publisher, William Randolph Hearst.

Let's pretend it is yesteryear, and we have been invited by Mr. Hearst to join him for dinner at his mansion. As we round the corner of La Cuesta Encantada—The Enchanted Hill—we catch our breath. Just look at those magnificent gardens, spacious pools, and exquisite statues! See the rambling walks adorned with fountains of fantasy and flowers of every color. And below us in the valley, exotic animals frolic in the world's largest private zoo.

Now we approach the castle itself with its thirty-eight bedrooms, fourteen sitting rooms and thirty-one bathrooms—100 rooms in all. And if that's not enough to impress you, the three adjacent guest houses boast an additional forty-six rooms.

Greeting us warmly, Mr. Hearst shows us around. First we go to the library, with its 5,000 rare books and fabulous collection of antique pottery. Next we pass to the game room, with its rare Gothic tapestry and antique Persian tiles. Then on to the private cinema. Mr. Hearst explains that many of the walls and ceilings surrounding us once graced the grand palaces of Europe.

But we must not linger. Dinner is ready. Entering the dining hall with its huge, crackling fireplace, we take our seats at 300-year-old monastery tables underneath silk banners from Italy. What a meal!

And what an evening! Finally our visit draws to a close at the incredible Roman pool. We gasp at the stunning sight of alabaster lamplight reflected in the water from thousands of eighteen-carat gold tiles.

Our visit over, we bid goodbye to Mr. Hearst and get back to daily living. But not for long. Jesus is coming soon to take us home to mansions far more glorious than any palace on earth!

One astonished guest at San Simeon remarked that it would take, not weeks or months, but perhaps years to examine all the treasures hoarded at the castle. And Hearst wasn't even finished! After three decades of work, he died with his pet project incomplete. And someday soon that beautiful castle, along with everything else on earth, will be destroyed by fire at the coming of the Lord Jesus Christ. But our mansions in heaven's Holy City will stand forever.

Here in Revelation 20 we'll learn more about God's wonderful plan for our future: "Blessed and holy is he who has part in the first resurrection. Over such the second death has no power, but they shall be priests of God and of Christ, and shall reign with Him a thousand years." Verse 6.

The raising of believers when Christ comes is called the first resurrection. At a second resurrection, those who rejected Jesus will face judgment and second death. We will learn about that in the next chapter.

So we will spend our first thousand years reigning with Christ in heaven. You know the beatitude, "Blessed are the poor in spirit, for theirs is the kingdom of heaven." Matthew 5:3. But Jesus also promised, "Blessed are the meek, for they shall inherit the earth." Matthew 5:5. Not this planet as we know it. A new earth, pure and unpolluted, redeemed from the ravages of sin, sickness, and death.

How will we take possession of this earth made new? Believe it or not, following our thousand years in heaven, we will move with the Holy City to earth. This is so incredible! I could not believe it if I had not seen it in the Bible. "And I saw a new heaven and a new earth, for the first heaven and the first earth had passed away. Also there was no more sea. Then I, John, saw the holy city, New Jerusalem, coming down out of heaven from God, prepared as a bride adorned for her husband. And I heard a loud voice from heaven saying, 'Behold, the tabernacle of God is with men, and He will dwell with them, and they shall be His people, and God Himself will be with them and be their God.' " Revelation 21:1-3.

Can you imagine what it will be like to move with the Holy City from heaven to earth? According to the Old Testament prophet Zechariah, Christ will stand that day upon the Mount of Olives, just outside the ruins of present Jerusalem. His feet will divide the mountain into a great plain on which the New Jerusalem will rest. And earth will be created anew before our very eyes!

Why would God move the capital city of the universe from heaven to our lowly planet? Simply because we are His special people. God so loved the world that He *gave* His beloved Son to this world. Jesus was not a loan but a gift. And He still belongs to us today. Forever our Saviour will be one of the human family, our brother as well as our Lord! The scripture we just read said, He "Himself will be with them and be their God." Remember?

And Jerusalem, where Jesus suffered and died for our sins, will be the place of God's eternal throne. Throughout ceaseless ages the citizens of the universe will worship with us at the site of our salvation.

We learn more about our new earth in Revelation 21: "And God will wipe away every tear from their eyes; there shall be no more death, nor sorrow, nor crying; and there shall be no more pain, for the former things have passed away. Then He who sat on the throne said, 'Behold, I make all things new.'" Verses 4, 5.

No more death! No more crying! No more pain! Goodbye arthritis and brain tumors! Farewell loneliness and disappointments! All things new with Jesus!

And there is more to explore about our eternal inheritance in the coming chapters. Meanwhile, remember that God will preserve our planet till the day of Christ's return. He will spare us from destroying ourselves by a global nuclear holocaust. Of course, it's possible some of our cities will be wiped out by warheads. We have already had Hiroshima and Nagasaki, you know. But Jesus said this world's buying and selling, building and planting, marrying and giving in marriage will continue uninterrupted until He breaks through the eastern sky.

I propose no political solution for the nuclear dilemma. Suppose the superpowers disarm all their warheads. That would be wonderful indeed! But it would hardly resolve the nuclear threat. Over twenty nations right now have nuclear capabilities. Some of them already have the bomb.

We have come to the point where positive thinking is irrational. What happens when terrorists flex muscles of megatons? A ten-kiloton device—just three kilotons less than the bomb that leveled Hiroshima—can fit inside a medium-size car. Can you imagine what one madman could do to Washington, D.C.? Sooner or later such a holocaust will happen—unless God intervenes.

No human cure exists for the troubles of this world. Instead, I point you to the promise of our Lord and Saviour—Jesus Christ: "I will come again."

Think about the glorious day of Christ's return. Think about it over and over. Let it give you something to live for. Could anything be more exciting to contemplate?

Seeing first a small, black cloud in the eastern sky. Watching it move nearer and nearer till it becomes a glorious white cloud. A cloud like none you've ever seen before. A cloud of angels— uncounted angels. Hearing a sound like none you have ever heard before. The sound of a trumpet echoing 'round the world. A voice like none you've heard before. The voice of the Lord Jesus calling the dead to life. The earth shaking. The tombs bursting open. Angels everywhere carrying little children from broken tombs to their mother's arms. Shouts of joy as loved ones long separated by death are reunited, never to part again!

And then, together with those resurrected ones, we who have waited through the long night are caught up into that angel starship, ready for the trip home.

I like to picture that space vehicle. A cloud of shining angels. A cloud chariot with living wings on either side. A rainbow above it and the appearance of fire beneath. Jesus riding the cloud—and not a person missed who really wanted to make the trip. Ten thousand angels surrounding the cloud and singing the praise of their Creator. Moving past the stars. A living starship on the way to the City of God!

I want to be there, don't you?

Meanwhile, God will take good care of us. So what if trouble and pain and disaster crowd our days and interrupt our nights? What if the wail of the siren is always with us—the whine of missiles, the roar of bombers, the thunder of approaching storms?

Let these simply remind us we have a better place to be and an absolutely fascinating way to get there. The great airlift, not by space shuttle, but by cloud to the city of our God!

Will your name be on the passenger list? It can be. There's only one requirement. It's the word *pardon,* written in the blood of the Lord Jesus Christ, beside your name. I urge you to permit Him to make your reservation today.

Hitler's Last Gasp

Auschwitz—Dachau—Ravensbrook—Nazi death camps.

Without a doubt the horror of modern history is the Holocaust. Hitler's massacre of innocent millions still staggers our understanding. Like smoke hovering over a furnace, unanswered questions linger on to haunt us. How did Hitler develop such gluttony for brutality? And what will God do to punish him?

Imagine, if you will, God asking your advice on judgment day. He wants you to help Him in deciding how to punish sinners. As you stand beside the great white throne, a man named Tom steps up to be judged. Years ago he discovered his wife at a motel hideaway with another lover. In a fit of jealous rage, Tom shot them both. One rash act. Otherwise, he lived a decent life. What sentence should Tom receive?

Next comes Karen, a shy teenager. Trembling in fear and shame, she tearfully admits to shoplifting a camera from K-Mart. How long should Karen suffer for her sin?

And now you meet that mastermind of mass extermination, Hitler himself. Little question that this monster of more than six million murders deserves to burn in hell. For a long time. A year maybe? Perhaps a thousand years?

Suppose God wants Hitler to burn forever for his incredible atrocities. You might understand that. But what if God also condemns Tom and Karen to suffer Hitler's fate? Sentencing all three to share eternity in the fire. No concern for their differing degrees of guilt. Does that sound fair?

71

Yet many teach that all sinners suffer the same sentence. That all burn in the flames of hell as long as time shall last. Forever and ever and ever. And that's not all. They believe God has been sending people to hell for thousands of years—beginning with Cain, who long ago killed his brother. Consider this. If Hitler went to hell when he died, even if he burns forever, he would still escape many centuries of the pain that Cain already suffered. Would that be just?

Would God punish sinners for centuries, only to call them up on judgment day to see whether they are really guilty? Tell me, friend, what kind of God do we have? Something is wrong here, wouldn't you say?

What's going on? Satan wants to make us hate our heavenly Father. So he twists the truth about God's love.

Let me read something written years ago. It may shock you."The sinner lies chained down on a bed of red-hot blazing fire. . . . The fire burns through every bone and every muscle, every nerve is trembling and quivering with the sharp fire. The fire rages inside the skull, it shoots out through the eyes, it roars in the throat as it roars up a chimney. So will mortal sin be punished . . . forever and ever!"

Believe it or not, this particular description of hell was published for the benefit of children. To make them respect God. "Incredible!" you gasp. Yes, indeed. God has been pictured as more savage than the worst terrorist—more cruel than the most bloodthirsty dictator!

Small wonder thousands have become unbelievers. They cannot connect the existence of a loving God with divine lust for endless torment. Robert Ingersoll, for example, might have become prince of preachers instead of foremost of infidels. But one day as a boy of ten he went with his father to hear a sermon on hell. The minister's demented descriptions incensed the lad. As young Ingersoll left the church, he turned and glared at his father. "If this is the kind of God we worship," the boy said between clenched teeth, "I want no part of Him. I hate Him!" Ingersoll's young heart could not handle such injustice. So that gifted intellect plunged over the cliff into unbelief.

Many today spurn such a revolting concept of God's wrath.

Only about half of Americans believe in a burning hell. Just 5 percent surveyed by the *Des Moines Register* and *Tribune* think they are headed for hellfire themselves. Of course, 31 percent are sure they know someone else is going to hell!

What does Scripture say about the fire? Once again we will probe the secrets of the Bible's last book. But first we must build a framework from other portions of God's Word.

In our last chapter, you may recall, we learned that those who die believing in Jesus will be resurrected at His coming. Then all of God's people travel together up to heaven to reign with Jesus for a thousand years.

Now we will study the future of those found unprepared when Jesus comes. "As it was in the days of Noah, so it will be also in the days of the Son of Man: They ate, they drank, they married wives, they were given in marriage, until the day that Noah entered the ark, and the flood came and destroyed them all." Luke 17:26, 27.

You know how it was in the days of Noah. Business as usual. Then came that fatal surprise from the clear blue sky. All who had neglected God's warning paid for it with their lives. So will it be when Jesus breaks through the eastern sky. Corpses will be scattered across the earth like driftwood.

Do you realize that one day soon, within the space of a few short hours, this earth will be depopulated—empty—with not one human being left alive, anywhere in the world? When God decides it's closing time, He will lock up this planet and leave it empty, uninhabited—without even a For Rent sign! We find a vivid picture of this desolate earth in the Old Testament book of Jeremiah.

We have all heard the gloomy predictions about how this world would look after a nuclear war. A dismal gray wasteland. Jeremiah's description of our planet after Jesus comes bears striking resemblance to the eerie scene scientists warn us about: "I beheld the earth, and indeed it was without form, and void; and the heavens, they had no light. I beheld the mountains, and indeed they trembled, and all the hills moved back and forth. I beheld, and indeed there was no man, and all the birds of the heavens had fled. I beheld, and indeed the fruitful land was a wilderness, and all its cities were broken down at the presence of the Lord, by His fierce anger. For thus says the Lord: 'The whole land shall be desolate; yet I will not make a full end.' " Jeremiah 4:23-27.

The prophet describes the earth as without form and void. Just as in the first chapter of Genesis, before Creation was complete. We also read that the earth will be dark. The heavens have no light. No human life remains; even the birds have fled.

Evidently sinners won't have a second chance. When Christ returns, all will have had their last chance. And that is it.

Is this morbid scene the final chapter of earth's history? No, friend, it is not. Did you notice the ray of hope? God promises, "Yet I will not make a full end." Evidently He still has plans for this planet.

Now, where will Satan spend the thousand years of earth's emptiness? In Revelation 20:1-3 we learn the devil will be exiled, confined to this earth with no one to tempt. "I saw an angel coming down from heaven, having the key to the bottomless pit and a great chain in his hand. He laid hold of the dragon, that serpent of old, who is the Devil and Satan, and bound him for a thousand years; and he cast him into the bottomless pit, and shut him up, and set a seal on him, so that he should deceive the nations no more till the thousand years were finished. But after these things he must be released for a little while."

There is no way to lock up Satan with a literal key or restrain him with a real chain. And no bottomless pit, no yawning chasm, could hold him. So what could this mean? Simply a symbolic way of saying that Satan will at last be stopped. He and his angels will be confined on this earth. Today Satan roams as a roaring lion, looking for people to devour with temptation. See 1 Peter 5:8. But after Jesus comes, every human being will be either dead or gone. The great rebel will have nothing to do for a thousand years. Except to wander over the dark, desolate earth amid the havoc he has caused.

But did you notice that the devil will be loosed again after his thousand-year vacation? This means he'll have his wicked followers back. We read on: "Now when the thousand years have expired, Satan will be released from his prison and will go out to deceive the nations which are in the four corners of the earth, Gog and Magog, to gather them together to battle, whose number is as the sand of the sea." Revelation 20:7, 8.

After the thousand years, things happen rapidly. Satan, loosed by the resurrection of the lost, once again controls the rebel host. What happens next? The drama unfolds in verse 9: "They went up on the breadth of the earth and surrounded the camp of the saints and the beloved city. And fire came down from God out of heaven and devoured them."

How did the Holy City, the camp of the saints get down here? Remember that in the last chapter we learned that the heavenly city, with all God's people in it, will travel through space to this planet. Then everyone who has ever lived will be alive, inside or outside the city.

Picture the scene. Satan compares the vast host under his command with the much smaller number within the city. Numbers favor his side. And he has military leaders from all history behind him. Hitler is there too. Satan rallies his forces for a final frenzied attack on God's throne. The vast rebel army advances toward the city.

Then what happens? Hell happens. Hell—as the Bible describes it—happens. Fire streaks down from above. The earth becomes a vast, seething lake of fire. But the city of God rides safely upon it—just as Noah's ark was protected during the waters of the Flood.

Hell will be hot. So hot, sin and sinners will not survive. But after those flames have done their work, they will go out. Just as the water receded in Noah's day, the lake of fire subsides. Then God brings beauty out of ashes. He restores this earth as beautiful as long-lost Eden. See 2 Peter 3:13.

Rebellion will be over, never to trouble a happy universe again. Sin will be gone—and with it death and pain and heartache. Finally Jesus fulfills His promise that the meek will inherit the earth. See Matthew 5:5. God will give this born-again planet to His people as their permanent home.

No eternally burning hell will pollute our new earth paradise. True, the *results* of hellfire will be eternal. There is no recovery from it—no resurrection from final, second death. But the suffering of the lost won't spoil our everlasting joy. Aren't you glad the lost will not suffer eternally?

These days many are urging stiffer punishment for criminals—even the death penalty for murderers. But I've never heard anyone suggest prolonged torture for any criminal, no matter how terrible the crime. Tell me, are we more kind than God? Sometimes I've wondered whether we feel that criminals themselves can be kinder than God.

Back in the summer of 1976, the people of Chowchilla, California, were stunned by the kidnapping of twenty-six local children. It happened at 4:15 the afternoon of July 15. Bus driver Ed Ray was returning with the children from a summer-school outing. Suddenly, up ahead, he saw a white van blocking the road. Ed hit the brakes and stopped. Three masked men, brandishing pistols and sawed-off shotguns, ordered him to the back of the bus with the children.

As you can imagine, the poor children were terrified. Some sat stunned. Others cried, pleaded, or fainted. Ed Ray tried to calm them down. But how could he hide his own fear? What were these masked men going to do with them?

Hiding the bus behind a thicket of tall bamboo, the kidnappers transferred the hostages into two vans. After a terrifying eleven-hour trip, they finally bumped to a stop. The bewildered, frightened children stumbled out. Guns pointed to a three-foot hole in the ground. They obeyed and Ed Ray was given a flashlight and forced in behind them. The hole was sealed with a metal plate, weighted down with giant truck batteries, and finally covered with dirt. The horrified captives were entombed alive!

Ed's flashlight showed that they were inside a buried moving van. The kidnappers had made quite elaborate preparations for their victims. Mattresses, Cheerios, potato chips, a couple of loaves of bread, and plenty of water. There were two improvised toilets. And, most important, two plastic ventilation pipes. Even fans.

The captives spent sixteen hours buried in their grave. Finally Ed, with the help of the boys, dug through to daylight. Ed Ray was a hero! And how Chowchilla cheered!

Listen. There are millions of Christians who think God is not as thoughtful as those kidnappers were. Are even some criminals kinder than God? Perish the thought!

Back in Noah's day, when the people drowned, they were gone. God did not keep them endlessly thrashing about in the water. And the citizens of Sodom and Gomorrah are not still burning there beneath the Dead Sea. But did you know the Bible says that the citizens of Sodom and Gomorrah were destroyed by "eternal fire"? Those are the very words. Listen. "Sodom and Gomorrah . . . are set forth as an example, suffering the vengeance of eternal fire." Jude 7.

Eternal fire. Eternal in its effect, you see. The *punishment* is everlasting—but not the *punishing*. Remember, the wages of sin is death. Not eternal life in hell. Death means the absence of life, the absence of existence. So the doctrine of eternal hell isn't seen in Scripture, no matter how many sincere people may have thought it to be so. It's tradition. A holdover from the Dark Ages.

Here is an interesting point to consider. On the cross, Jesus paid the wages of the whole world's sin by His death. Didn't He? Certainly! Did He suffer eternal torment? Of course not. Then to say sinners must be eternally punished suggests that Jesus failed to pay the full price of their sin. And we know that is not true!

Those who reject their Saviour's death will finally perish. For the good of the universe, for the good of everyone concerned, every trace of sin will be erased. God's eternal kingdom of peace will reign at last.

But what does the Bible mean about the smoke of their torment ascending up forever? Allow Scripture to explain its own terms. Did you know the Bible uses the word *forever* more than fifty times for things already ended? For instance, in 1 Samuel 1:22, we read that Hannah promised Samuel to the Lord "forever." Yet verse 28 explains, "As long as he lives he shall be lent to the Lord."

There you have it. As long as the wicked live, as long as consciousness lasts, they will burn. For some it may be just a few moments. Others will suffer longer. Yet even Hitler will finally heave his last gasp. Satan himself will perish at the end of the thousand years. That is what the record says. "You. . . shall be no more forever." Ezekiel 28:19.

You may wonder, "Why does God wait a thousand years to dispense with sin?" Simply this. God will not destroy the wicked until all the universe fully understands why—until you and I understand. So Paul speaks of a time when "the saints will judge the world." Remember? 1 Corinthians 6:2. During our thousand years in heaven, we will have time to examine God's dealings with loved ones who were lost. We will see God has indeed done all He could do to save each person. Then we will be prepared to witness the solemn and awful judgment of the lost.

Friend, think of the disappointment in the heart of the Saviour if you should be missing. No one could take your place. Not all the millions of the saved. Not all the adoring angels. Your Heavenly Father needs you there. Don't disappoint Him!

How God's heart will be crushed on the day of hellfire! Long ago Jesus cried over a doomed city. "O Jerusalem, Jerusalem . . . ! How often I wanted to gather your children together, as a hen gathers her chicks under her wings, but you were not willing!" Matthew 23:37.

"O New York, how often I have stood beside your spires of steel and called out over Times Square and Broadway, but you would not hear!

"O London, how often My voice has blended with that of Big Ben, tolling the lateness of the hour. But you ignored My warning.

"O precious planet in rebellion, how patiently I have knocked at your hearts' doors, urging you to let Me in. I tried to save you from the burning. Yet you weren't willing! Now it's too late!"

But friend, today there's still time. Whether you realize it or not, this moment you are deciding whether to be inside or outside the Holy City. You do not have to be locked outside with Satan when the fire falls. You can be safely inside with the Lord Jesus Christ!

I think of the Australian lumberman who built a little cabin at the edge of the woods. One evening as he returned from work, a horrible scene met his sight. A forest fire had swept through and destroyed his little home. Only a smoking heap remained.

He wandered out to where the old chicken coop had stood. It too was a mass of ashes and burned wire. At his feet lay a mound of charred feathers. He idly kicked it over. And what do you suppose happened? Four little fuzzy babies scrambled out. Four little chicks survived, sheltered by their mother's love.

Friend, do you want to be covered when fire sweeps through this planet? You can be. You can be sheltered in your Saviour now.

Mutiny in Paradise

Starving babies. Orphaned children. Weeping widows. War-torn nations.

"If God is love—why?"

From countless broken hearts around the world comes the anguished cry, the angry demand, "Why, God? If You really love us, why don't You help us? If You are all powerful, why won't You stop our suffering? How did we ever get into this mess?"

Disturbing questions! Vital questions that deserve sane answers. Answers we will find in Revelation, the last book of the Bible.

So we launch into our fourth chapter focusing on the prophecies of Revelation. We will explore the story behind the great battle between good and evil raging throughout the prophecies of this fascinating book.

Really, this world did not have to turn out the way it did. Back in the beginning, when God gave us the Garden of Eden, there were no weapons. No pollutants. No prisons or hospitals. No need for soldiers or policemen—or preachers either! This planet emerged from its Creator's hand pure and perfect. And it was built to stay that way.

Well, whatever happened? It is the story of a planet in rebellion. A rebellion on earth that began with war in heaven. Yes— war in heaven, of all places! Let's read it now in Revelation 12:7-9. "War broke out in heaven: Michael and his angels fought against the dragon; and the dragon and his angels

81

fought, but they did not prevail, nor was a place found for them in heaven any longer. So the great dragon was cast out, that serpent of old, called the Devil and Satan, who deceives the whole world; he was cast to the earth, and his angels were cast out with him."

Can you picture this cosmic drama? A mutiny in heaven! A revolt by Satan and his angels against the government of God. But the rebellion failed. The devil and his hosts were thrown out of heaven to this earth. But how did Satan come into existence in the first place? And where did he get his wicked angels? Did God create evil?

No. God created a perfect angel named Lucifer, who became the devil by his own choice. We find the story in Ezekiel chapter 28: "You were the anointed cherub who covers; I established you; you were on the holy mountain of God; you walked back and forth in the midst of fiery stones. You were perfect in your ways from the day you were created, till iniquity was found in you." "Your heart was lifted up because of your beauty; you corrupted your wisdom for the sake of your splendor; I cast you to the ground." Verses 14, 15, 17.

Do you see what happened? Lucifer, the one God anointed as head of the angels, became proud of himself. He abused the influence of his high authority to stir up trouble. So great were his deceptions that one third of heaven's angels joined his revolt. See Revelation 12:4.

How could a perfect angel start a rebellion? Was something wrong in the way God created Lucifer? No, rather, it was because God gave him freedom—power to choose his own way. God could have created a robot, programmed to be a puppet and obey without second thought. Or any thought at all. But God wouldn't do that. He loves His family and craves our willing love in return. And love cannot be commanded or programmed. We respond by free choice in appreciation of God's love.

Just as there can be no love without freedom, there can be no freedom without risk. Freedom brings opportunity for abuse. The same freedom that offers love can withhold it. The same exercise of choice that obeys can rebel. A dangerous risk indeed, this power to choose. But God was willing to risk His very throne for the sake of our freedom and love.

As Lucifer's insurrection ripened into active revolt, he attacked the throne of God. We read about it in Isaiah 14, beginning with verse 12: "How you are fallen from heaven, O Lucifer, son of the morning! How you are cut down to the ground. You who weakened the nations! For you have said in your heart: 'I will ascend into heaven, I will exalt my throne above the stars of God; I will also sit on the mount of the congregation on the farthest sides of the north; I will ascend above the heights of the clouds, I will be like the Most High.'" Verses 12-14.

For the good of the universe, God could not allow such a selfish tyrant to prevail in his power play. So He cast the devil out of heaven into exile on this planet. But why didn't God destroy the rebellion then and there? He could have saved Himself a lot of trouble. He could have saved Himself the cross!

But no, God let His rival live on for the benefit of the universe. Satan had claimed to offer a better government. The only way to expose this lie was to give the rebel the opportunity to prove his point and develop his principles. Only then could the universe fully see that God's way is best, that suffering and death await those who stray from His love.

Why was Satan exiled here, of all places? Because this world was soon to become the theater of the universe. God had a special plan for this planet. He wanted to populate our globe with human beings created in His image. God had many angels for company, but now He needed to start a family.

It shouldn't be hard for us to understand why God wanted children. What makes a couple with a double income interrupt their peace and prosperity for a precious, lovable, but sometimes restless little troublemaker? We may have friends, as God had angels, yet there's a hunger to have and hold children created in our image. A craving to love and care for our very own offspring. That's why God made us in His image, to somehow bear His likeness.

The Bible tells us that God breathed into Adam's nostrils the breath of life. Can't you picture our heavenly Father bending over His beloved offspring, tenderly sharing His own life?

By creating humanity in His image, God gave us freedom of choice. Not to ride the rail of His will like a locomotive, without a way of our own. Rather, as free moral agents, He gave us a steering wheel—the ability to do as we please. God knew we couldn't be happy unless we were free. And only through this freedom could we respond to His love.

In making us in His image, God took a further risk. He also gave us dominion—the responsibility to care for children of our own. You see the danger in this. Because if we ever went astray, everyone around us would suffer. A terrible risk indeed, this responsibility for others. But God knew we wouldn't feel fulfilled without it.

Then our Father lavished the finest that heaven could bestow upon His human family. He spared nothing. Picture the lush green meadows sprinkled with a rainbow of flowers. Rich fragrant forests. Clear running streams. The tree of life. And the other tree—the tree that offered death.

Why did God plant that tree of temptation there? To trap Adam and Eve? No. God presented this tree as a test of their trust and loyalty. He assured them that everything that could make them happy was already theirs through Him. But if they ever wished to doubt His leadership, someone else offered another option. Satan the serpent was eager to lure them away from their Father's love. The choice was theirs.

And the stakes were high. It was a life-or-death matter. If they ever left God, they would die, He warned. This was no arbitrary sentence. It was a basic fact of life. God is not only the Author but the Sustainer of life. Cut off from their source, humanity would have no more existence than a tree branch severed from its trunk. And if they sinned, the whole human race would be doomed. All their children and their children's children would be plunged into the grave.

And one sad day, it happened. You know the story. Our first parents succumbed to the fatal delusion that something was lacking in God's care, that God had withheld what the serpent would supply. Suddenly the relationship was shattered! God's precious children became strangers and orphans. By their own choice!

Sin took an immediate toll. Alienation and discord displaced harmony and happiness. Adam and Eve hid from God—or tried to. Reluctantly, God reminded them that they would have to die.

But then He surprised them with some good news which we call the gospel. Death would have to be, yes. But He would take their death upon Himself. He would pay the price with His own blood.

They must leave their garden home, but God would join them in their exile. Sweat and pain would be their lot, but God would hold their hands. And in the course of time He would come to this planet on His high-risk rescue mission.

How did He do it?

Jesus left the throne of heaven to be planted in the womb of a peasant girl. Imagine! The mighty Creator God became a creature, locked into time and space. Actually, it was God who worked in the carpenter's shop and joined our rat race. It was God who lived in poverty, who felt thirst from the noonday heat. It was God who got tired and slept in the storm-tossed boat. And it was all because He loved us and needed our friendship.

What kind of reception did God receive from us? The New Testament records the sad story that His own people refused to receive Him. Bitter disappointment! Yes, large crowds followed the Lord, but they mostly wanted to see His miracles and be healed of pain. Very few cared about His friendship.

A few disciples faithfully followed Him, but even they were too involved in their own power struggles to appreciate that God Himself was walking, talking, and sleeping with them. The night before His death, they argued about which of them ranked number one. They didn't even listen as Jesus tried to discuss His sacrifice for them the next morning. He had to wash their feet like a servant to win their attention and show them what it meant to be great.

The crisis occurred later that night in a garden called Gethsemane. Let's watch Jesus as He collapses under a deadly oppression which threatens to snuff out His life.

What is this strange smog choking His soul? It's the guilt of

our sin. Our sins are clogging the lifeline with His Father that
has sustained the Saviour on earth. As He ponders the price to
be paid, He falls on His face in prayer: "My Father, if it's possible, take this cup of suffering away from Me! Yet not what I
want—may Your will be done. But Father, if there's any other
way We can save them, tell Me!" See Luke 22:42.

There isn't. So a crucial decision must now be made in the
moonlit garden. Will He go through with it all? Or should
guilty humanity bear its own deserved punishment?

Desperately needing the support of His disciples, He begs
them to pray for Him. But they don't seem concerned. Worn out
from their arguing, they fall fast asleep. Three times our Lord
staggers back to hear some word of support or encouragement
that the sacrifice of His soul would not be wasted. But each
time He is greeted by their insensitive sleeping.

What pressure to give up and go back to heaven! And why
not? His enemies are on the march to arrest Him. His friends
don't seem to care. What good would it do to sacrifice Himself?

As Christ ponders what to do, the fate of humanity trembles
in the balance. Finally, amid the bitterest agony, He makes the
decision. Jesus will go to the cross! He will suffer the wrath of
divine justice and satanic torment. He will pass through the
grave to restore the shattered relationship with His sinful children.

As the mob makes its midnight arrest, the sleeping disciples
awake. They get up and run away. All of them flee for their
lives. Now the Son of God allows Himself to be handcuffed and
rushed to court. There His enemies—those He came to save—
condemn Him in the greatest travesty of justice this world has
ever seen.

After being scourged till the blood spurts out, Christ is led
away to a most painful and shameful death. His clothes are
torn from Him. Now He hangs in open shame on the cruel cross.
Maddened tormentors jeer the bleeding Lord as He writhes in
agony. But far worse than the physical torment is the separation from His Father for our sin. In sheer terror He cries, "My
God, My God, why have You forsaken Me?"

Why, God? Jesus wonders too!

Tell me, friend, Why *did* the Father in heaven have to forsake His Son? So He could accept you and me! Listen to this sublime passage from Ellen White's inspired book *The Desire of Ages,* pp. 755, 756.

"The spotless Son of God hung upon the cross, His flesh lacerated with stripes; those hands so often reached out in blessing, nailed to the wooden bars; those feet so tireless on ministries of love, spiked to the tree; that royal head pierced by the crown of thorns; those quivering lips shaped to the cry of woe. And all that He endured—the blood drops that flowed from His head, His hands, His feet, the agony that racked His frame, and the unutterable anguish that filled His soul at the hiding of His Father's face—speaks to each child of humanity, declaring, it is for thee that the Son of God consents to bear this burden of guilt; for thee He spoils the domain of death, and opens the gates of Paradise. He who stilled the angry waves and walked the foam-capped billows, who made devils tremble and disease flee, who opened blind eyes and called forth the dead to life— offers Himself upon the cross as a sacrifice, and this from love to thee. He, the Sin Bearer, endures the wrath of divine justice, and for thy sake becomes sin itself."

Christ had done no wrong. But as our stand-in and substitute, He took our punishment. He was pronounced guilty, so we could be declared forgiven and live with Him forever.

Christ is crucified between two thieves. They join the crowd in hurling insults at the Saviour. But one of them begins to realize that something out of place is happening. Someone innocent is dying—a Saviour dying for his own sin. Hope springs within his breast. Maybe it's not too late! Desperately he casts himself upon the mercy of the One he so recently mocked. Quickly, acceptance comes. The dying Saviour promises a place in paradise to a dying thief.

As Jesus dies, He declares in triumph, "It is finished!" Mission accomplished! Humanity redeemed! Children of God again!

No more fearful hiding, like Adam and Eve in the shame of their sin. We've been adopted! Our heavenly Father wants us home. Will you come? Will you accept His gift of salvation as more precious than anything else you know? The choice is yours.

By His life and death, Christ won back all that was lost. Soon He will restore everything the human race once enjoyed in Eden. Let's take a few moments as we close our study to preview the paradise home Jesus promised. You'll find the description in Revelation 21, verses 1 to 5:

"And I saw a new heaven and a new earth, for the first heaven and the first earth had passed away. Also there was no more sea. Then I, John, saw the holy city, New Jerusalem, coming down out of heaven from God, prepared as a bride adorned for her husband. And I heard a loud voice from heaven saying, 'Behold, the tabernacle of God is with men, and He will dwell with them, and they shall be His people, and God Himself will be with them and be their God. And God will wipe every tear from their eyes; there shall be no more death, nor sorrow, nor crying; and there shall be no more pain, for the former things have passed away.' Then He that sat on the throne said, 'Behold, I make all things new.' "

Think of it, friend—all things new! And it's all for you! What are you going to do about it?

As we consider our response to God's love, I'm reminded of the little poodle who felt trapped inside his master's house. Envying the kids outside building a snowman, he longs for an opportunity to run free. Finally he manages to slip out the door.

Delighted to be loose at last, he dashes back and forth across the yard and around and around the snowman. But soon his little legs get cold. His enthusiasm shivers away. Finally he concludes that, be it ever so humdrum, there's no place like home. Its confinement offers warmth and security. Colder and wiser, he whimpers on the doorstep. Of course, his master lets the repentant little fellow back inside.

Tell me, friend, are you like that poodle? Tired of running in circles outside the Father's warm house? Shivering with guilt and shame? Then come inside your heavenly Father's house where it's warm. Live in His love and be safe evermore.

When the Red Phone Rings

October 1962. A crisis over Cuba. Enemy missiles lurking in America's front yard!

President Kennedy responds with a daring naval blockade. Yet Soviet ships steam relentlessly forward. It's a terrifying superpower showdown! Suddenly we find ourselves poised on the brink of World War III. The world holds its breath. Finally the Russians back down.

It was a narrow escape. But what will happen next time?

After the close call over Cuba, both superpowers saw the need for directly communicating in a crisis. Instantly. Accurately. So in August of 1963 they linked Washington and Moscow with a hotline.

The red phone, as we call it now, has served us well. Its first use came in 1967 during the Six-Day War. During the next clash between the Arabs and Israelis, the hotline buzzed again. Few Americans understood the danger of that October 1973 crisis. How close the superpowers edged toward war.

We still depend upon the hotline. It is our last resort against doomsday. Do you recall Walter Mondale's campaign commercial with the ringing red phone? His point was that America needs experienced leadership to avoid nuclear war.

Of course, we need leaders we can trust. But who really runs the red phone? We've been to the brink of World War III time and again. Yet business continues as usual. Is some supernatural power holding back the winds of strife? If so, for how long?

In Revelation 7, beginning with verse 1, we find out.

"After these things I saw four angels standing at the four corners of the earth, holding the four winds of the earth, that the wind should not blow on the earth, on the sea, or on any tree. Then I saw another angel ascending from the east, having the seal of the living God. And he cried with a loud voice to the four angels to whom it was granted to harm the earth and the sea, saying, 'Do not harm the earth, the sea, or the trees till we have sealed the servants of our God on their foreheads.' " Revelation 7:1-3.

Winds on a leash! Angels holding back the winds of war and destruction. Containing the nuclear threat. Forbidding history to sign out just yet.

Why does God delay the end of the world? Because something must first happen with His people. We must receive the seal of the living God before Jesus comes. Evidently this business of being sealed is pretty important. Shall we probe it further?

Revelation 7 goes on to describe how 144,000 saints will be sealed. Twelve thousand from each of the twelve tribes of Israel.

This number twelve shows completeness. A complete year has twelve months. Christ called twelve apostles. The Holy City has twelve pearly gates. And Old Testament Israel began with twelve distinct tribes.

But then the various tribes intermarried among themselves. Today it would probably be impossible to find exactly 12,000 pure-blooded members of each of the old twelve tribes. So this reference to Israel must be symbolic. Who are the real children of Israel now?

According to the New Testament, believers in Jesus are God's chosen people. Not through their national origin. But because of their faith in Christ. All God's promises to Abraham belong to Christians today. In Jesus we become the new Israel. See Galatians 3:29.

So the symbolic 144,000 Israelites, or God's followers actually, represent the complete family of all believers at the end of the world. The great multitude from all nations who overcome earth's final crisis. Those who receive God's seal.

A friend of mine shared a personal experience that helps me

understand what it means to be sealed. As a boy he attended a little country school. Thirteen students in eight grades in one room. The teacher was a seventeen-year-old girl, fresh out of school. As you can imagine, she had her hands full keeping law and order. Soon her struggle became a losing battle.

One afternoon outside the schoolhouse my friend joined his peers in complaining about classes. He voiced his dislike for the teacher. How much he hated her rules. How much he wished she would go away.

Just then he happened to glance through the open window. There stood that poor teacher, her shoulders quivering with sobs. The sight of her sorrow pierced him like a sword. He realized now that misbehavior meant more than breaking a rule. He had broken a heart. Overwhelmed with remorse and repentance, he determined to become a new boy. And he did!

Friend, this is the experience of God's people who are sealed. They have learned that indulging in sin means more than breaking God's law. It also breaks His heart. And they resolve to die rather than do that. We see this attitude of God's people in Hebrews 8. Let's read verse 10.

" 'This is the covenant that I will make with the house of Israel: After those days,' says the Lord, 'I will put My laws in their mind and write them on their hearts; and I will be their God, and they shall be My people.' " Hebrews 8:10.

A willing mind in harmony with God's law. This is what it means to have heaven's seal upon your forehead.

Come with me back to Revelation. In chapter 14 we meet the symbolic 144,000 again. This time they have God's name on their foreheads. In Bible days parents chose names to represent the character they wanted their children to have. Today we usually pick names to honor relatives or other favorite people. Or we like the sound of the name. But whether we know it or not, even now each name has its own special meaning.

Can you guess what my name, George, means? "Tiller of the ground. Farmer." My wife Nellie's name means "possessor of feminine virtues." What does your name mean? Go down to the library sometime and look it up. See whether your name actually represents your character.

The sealed saints who bear God's name reflect His character. His faithful love. They are not defiled by hypocrisy. Instead they remain pure as virgins in their relationship with God. And they obey His commandments. Notice verse 12: "Here is the patience of the saints; here are those who keep the commandments of God and the faith of Jesus."

Faith in Jesus. Keeping God's commandments. They go together in receiving the seal. God waits while we learn how to trust and obey. We discover more about these sealed saints in the message they believe. Revelation 14, verses 6 and 7:

"I saw another angel flying in the midst of heaven, having the everlasting gospel to preach to those who dwell on the earth—to every nation, tribe, tongue, and people—saying with a loud voice, 'Fear God and give glory to Him, for the hour of His judgment has come; and worship Him who made heaven and earth, the sea and springs of water.' "

An angel with a message. Calling the whole world to worship the Creator. To prepare for judgment. To accept salvation.

Some say the gospel belongs to the New Testament. But notice that it is called the "everlasting gospel." It has been with us from the day sin invaded our planet.

Picture the scene in the Garden of Eden. Adam and Eve linger under the tree, savoring the flavor of forbidden fruit. Suddenly chills race up their spines. Icy pangs of guilt and shame. Shivering in their nakedness, they hunt for refuge in the depths of the forest. As they crouch amid their lush green prison, terror overwhelms them. They remember God's warning. On the day they sinned, they must die. And here He comes to kill them!

But no. God doesn't strike them dead. Instead, He tenderly covers their shame with the skin of an animal. What is happening here? Why does He let them live?

Or did they really die that day after all? Think this through. What must you do to get a garment of skin? You must kill. An innocent animal, probably a lamb, perished in place of the condemned couple. Because a substitute died their death, they could live. A happy life, free from shame and guilt.

You know who that substitute symbolized. Our Lord Jesus

Christ, the great Lamb of God. He offers us salvation as a gift. Free, but not cheap. It cost His death on the cross.

This is the everlasting gospel. The foundation of Christianity. And we found it way back at the gates of Eden.

Like a refreshing mountain stream, the gospel runs clear through the Old Testament. Take the experience of Abraham and his son Isaac. As they trudge up Mount Moriah, the mountain of sacrifice, the aged father trembles at the thought of losing his only son. Then he remembers the gospel: "My son, God will provide for Himself the lamb for a burnt offering." Genesis 22:8. God Himself provides the sacrifice for sin. That was their hope way back in Genesis! And that is our hope today.

Unfortunately, Abraham's descendants forgot the gospel. So God brought them to Mount Sinai and taught them the meaning of sacrifice. Every bleeding lamb on the altar reminded them to trust in the blood of their Saviour to come.

At Mount Sinai God reminded them of something else. We find it in Exodus 20. Way back at creation, God had given His children a weekly reminder to trust in Him. Let's read about it, beginning with verse 8: "Remember the Sabbath day, to keep it holy. Six days you shall labor and do all your work, but the seventh day is the Sabbath of the Lord your God. In it you shall do no work. . . . For in six days the Lord made the heavens and the earth, the sea, and all that is in them, and rested the seventh day. Therefore the Lord blessed the Sabbath day and hallowed it." Verses 8-11.

"Remember the Sabbath." Why? Because the Sabbath calls us to cease from our works and rest in God's work for us. He finished creation in six days and rested the seventh. Then He invited His children—who deserved nothing—to share the celebration of His work.

The Sabbath commandment differs from the other nine. All the other commandments tell us what we must do for God and neighbor. But the Sabbath points us away from human works. To rest in God's work for us. And that's the gospel! Without Sabbath rest, our obedience would be legalism.

Come reverently with me now to Calvary. It's late Friday afternoon, almost time to welcome the Sabbath. Jesus, hanging on the cross, recalls all He has done for our salvation. Then, with His dying breath, He proclaims, "It is finished!" Mission accomplished! Mankind redeemed!

Again Jesus rests from His work on the Sabbath, just as He did after creation. Only this time in the tomb. Following Sabbath rest, Christ arises and ascends to heaven's throne.

Can you see how the Sabbath is the greatest teaching tool of the gospel? The brightest of billboards proclaiming Calvary's freedom? Week by week it reminds us that we can't save ourselves—we must trust Jesus. And in this world cursed by atheism, the Sabbath testifies that we didn't evolve by chance. God created us. We're His children.

We turn now to Exodus 31. Can you see why Jesus proclaimed Himself "Lord of the Sabbath"? Because it commemorates His two greatest acts on our behalf—creating us and saving us. We show our faith in Jesus, our Maker and Redeemer, by resting on the seventh day. The Sabbath seals our relationship with Him. We see this here in verse 13: "Surely My Sabbaths you shall keep, for it is a sign between Me and you throughout your generations, that you may know that I am the Lord who sanctifies you."

So the Sabbath is the sign between God and His people. At creation God "sanctified" the seventh day. That is, He set it apart from other days of the week. And now, through the Sabbath, God sets us apart from the world to seal us as His own.

But most of us don't want to be set apart from the world. We would rather fit in with the crowd. Why this strange urge to conform?

Why are we terrified about being different? Where is the fervent individualism that made the heroes and the martyrs of the past? What happened to the excitement of taking one's stand? We seem to be hypnotized with the childhood game of follow-the-leader.

Margaret Applegarth has written a delightful book called *Men as Trees Walking*. In it she tells the story, true but almost unbelievable, of Jean Henri Fabre and his study of the processionary caterpillar.

It seems that this caterpillar wanders about aimlessly, pursued by many followers who move when he moves, stop when he stops, and eat when he eats. Pine needles are their principal source of food.

One day Fabre tried an experiment. He filled a flowerpot with pine needles, which they love, and then lined up the caterpillars in a solid ring around the rim of the pot. Sure enough, they began to move slowly around and around the rim, each following the one ahead. And yes, you've guessed it. They continued this senseless revolving for seven days, never once stopping for food—until one by one they began to collapse.

No. It is not always safe to follow the crowd. To have followed the public mood in Christ's day would have been to reject Him. Listen to the report of the officers sent out to arrest Jesus, but returning without Him. "The officers answered, 'No man ever spoke like this Man!' Then the Pharisees answered them, 'Are you also deceived? Have any of the rulers or the Pharisees believed in Him?' " John 7:46-48.

This was the question that discouraged so many from following Jesus. They had been deeply moved by Christ's message. But when reminded that the religious leaders had rejected Him, they surrendered conscience and forfeited faith. Do we have that problem today?

Truth still burns its conviction into human hearts. It may be startling truth. It may seem strange to modern ears. It may concern the day God says to remember. And there are those who ask, "Have the respected leaders of our day accepted it? Has it been received into the mainstream of religious thought?"

Sabbath rest, you see, sets God's people apart from the world. You might say it keeps us from becoming processionary caterpillars! Not that the seventh day has any value in itself. It's rather what the day represents. Let me illustrate what I mean.

Take a piece of red cloth. It's not worth much by itself. But add some white cloth and some blue cloth and sew them all together into the Tricolor of France. Frenchmen will die for their flag! Sew them together into the Union Jack, and Britishers will lay down their lives for it. And if you sew those ordinary pieces of cloth into the Stars and Stripes, Americans will die for it!

Just so, God took an ordinary day. But then He set it apart from other days of the week and made the Sabbath. He made it represent the greatest things He's done for us. The reasons why we worship Him.

Remember that angel's message in Revelation 14? It repeats the very words of the Sabbath commandment: "Worship Him who made heaven and earth."

So the Sabbath stands at the foundation of true worship. A test of our willingness to serve God.

You can imagine how Satan hates the Sabbath. Because it is the sign of our relationship with God. And the devil does not want us to be sealed. He does not want us to be free.

Back in the old days, on the shores of the Mississippi, Abraham Lincoln stood near the market for slave trading. He watched the tragic sight of families torn apart. Their heartbreaking sobs pierced his soul. Clenching his fists, he vowed, "If I ever get a chance to hit this, I'll hit it hard." And he did.

Before Lincoln's great emancipation, a slave named Joe was shoved on the auction block. Bitter and resentful, he muttered, "I won't work! I won't work!" But a wealthy landowner purchased him anyway.

He led Joe to the carriage, and they drove out of town to the plantation. There by a lake stood a little bungalow. With curtains, flowers, and a cobblestone walkway. The new master stopped the carriage. Turning to Joe, he smiled. "Here's your new home. You don't have to work for it. I've bought you to set you free."

For a moment Joe sat stunned. Then his eyes filled with tears. Overwhelmed, he exclaimed, "Master, I'll serve you forever."

Long ago Someone from a land far away looked down on this earth. He saw our bondage to Satan and heard our cry for freedom. He determined, "Someday I'll get a chance to hit that, and I'll hit it hard." And Jesus did. By His death He set us free.

And He has prepared a wonderful place for us. Beautiful beyond our wildest imagination. Soon He will return to take us home. To be with Him forever.

Oh, friend. Will you serve Him forever?

The Antichrist Exposed

The antichrist. We've been warned, and we've been waiting. Who in the world will it be? A religious fanatic like the Ayatollah Khomeini? Or a political tyrant like Idi Amin? A cult leader such as Sun Myung Moon? Perhaps an atheist like Madalyn Murray O'Hair?

The antichrist. Is it a human or a demon? A government? Maybe even a church?

Fascinated and frightened. That's how we feel about the mysteries of the antichrist. We're also quite confused. Bookstores, even drugstores, feature a smorgasbord of paperback religious thrillers. Each comes spiced with new speculation about the beast.

How can we know what's truth? We'd better get the facts straight from the source, wouldn't you say? Why don't we open our Bibles to Revelation 13—the so-called "beast chapter." Let's read chapter 13, verses 1 and 2:

"I stood on the sand of the sea. And I saw a beast rising up out of the sea, having seven heads and ten horns, and on his horns ten crowns, and on his heads a blasphemous name. Now the beast which I saw was like a leopard, his feet were like the feet of a bear, and his mouth like the mouth of a lion. And the dragon gave him his power, his throne, and great authority."

A strange beast indeed, this antichrist power. With a body from a leopard, a bear, and a lion. Perhaps you've studied those animals before in the Old Testament book of Daniel. We learn from Scripture decoding that they represent three kingdoms—

97

three ancient kingdoms, in fact—Babylon, Persia, and Greece. Followed, of course, by the Roman Empire.

So this blasphemous beast of Revelation 13 sums up the great world empires of Old Testament history. What religion did those heathen empires have in common? Sun worship.

Adoration of the sun can be traced all the way back to the time of Noah. Nimrod, his great-grandson, became a "mighty one on the earth." Genesis 10:8. Beginning with his Tower of Babel, Nimrod's achievements adorn the records and legends of ancient history. But this talented leader was evil. A father of false worship.

False worship also thrived through Ishtar, called the queen of heaven, goddess of love and fertility. Ishtar, according to legend, gave birth to a son Tammuz, without a father. Here in pagan sun worship, centuries before Christ, we find a counterfeit of the virgin birth. Imagine! Certain of the male gods of fertility became sun gods. They all died every winter and had to be resurrected to restore the fertility of plants, animals, and humans.

Sun worship from ancient Babylon spread to infect the world. Ancient records and art forms show how each nation reverenced the sun in the customs of its own culture. But why did they worship the sun? Well, the sun brings light, warmth, growth—what we need for life itself. Reigning supreme over nature, the sun would be the natural object of worship for those who reject their Creator.

Ceremonies to honor the sun god were gruesome beyond belief. Babies were burned as living sacrifices. Young women were degraded as sun temple prostitutes. All to appease the endless appetite of sun dieties rather than to accept the Creator's gift of salvation.

Time and again God exposed the follies of sun worship. Remember the story of how He rescued His people from Egypt? How He overpowered the sun with three days of darkness? All who turned from the sun god and put the lamb's blood on their doorpost were saved from the death angel. Even so, Israel exported sun idolatry in the Exodus. The golden calf they reverenced represented Apis, an image closely associated with sun worship.

Throughout Old Testament times adoration of the sun supplanted true worship in Israel. King Solomon, the very one who built God's temple, defiled Jerusalem with paganism. Sun worship flourished. The eighth chapter of Ezekiel records the shocking scene of women reverencing Tammuz in the temple. And men bowing low before the sun.

Can you imagine! Pagan worship in God's own temple! But faithful prophets called Israel away from the sun to their Creator. They pointed to the seventh-day Sabbath, God's weekly reminder of Creation. Yet the Hebrews persisted in paganism. Finally the Lord gave them up to be captives in Babylon, that ancient center of sun worship. At last God's people learned their lesson.

But they then went to the other extreme. After returning from Babylon, they shunned their pagan neighbors to avoid contamination. By the time of Christ, the Jews had largely quarantined themselves from the Gentiles around them.

Meanwhile, after Babylon fell to the Persians, sun worship continued to spread. And when Alexander the Great conquered the then-known world, the Greeks introduced their own sophisticated brand of idolatry. Including reverence for the sun.

And, of course, the Romans venerated the sun in their empire. They named the days of the week according to their heathen religion. Sunday they reverenced the sun. Monday the Moon. Tuesday, Mars. Wednesday, Mercury. Thursday they honored Jupiter. Friday, Venus. Saturday? You guessed it—Saturn. Just as the sun rules over the planets, Sunday rose to honor above other days in the week.

But true Christians of the first century nobly refused any part of pagan worship. And as a result they suffered horrible persecution. Thousands were thrown to the lions or burned alive. Yet the church stood firm. Satan, failing to overcome God's people through force, then tried a new strategy. He determined to infiltrate Christianity through paganism. Little by little he mingled the ceremonies of sun worship with Bible truth.

Now why would the church be attracted to paganism? For one thing, Christians wanted to distance themselves from anything seeming to be Jewish. Jews, you see, had put themselves in the emperor's doghouse. They hated Roman authority. Constantly they revolted to regain their own national rule.

And Rome struck back. In A.D. 49 Emperor Claudius expelled the Jews from Rome for their constant rioting. See Acts 18:2. Things got worse. Strict sanctions were enjoined upon Jews. They responded by refusing to pray for God's blessing on the emperor. Rome considered this treason.

So in A.D. 70 Roman armies stormed Jerusalem. A quarter of a million Jews were starved, burned, crucified, or otherwise killed. Their glorious temple lay in ruins. Numerous anti-Jewish riots swept the empire, climaxed by even stiffer penalties for Jews.

You see, because Christians shared the same heritage as Jews, Romans tended to treat both groups the same. This was unfair, of course. Christians wanted peace with the emperor, rendering to Caesar his due. Yet they suffered just as if they were Jews. No wonder Christians cut themselves off from everything remotely Jewish. You can see why they craved a new identity more favorable with the empire.

And now with Jerusalem destroyed, Christians looked to the capital city as their new church center. By A.D. 95 Clement, bishop of Rome, had become quite prominent. His epistles commanded respect among believers. Some in the churches even considered them inspired. Rome's influence in the church increased further after the second destruction of Jerusalem in A.D. 135. Emperor Hadrian outlawed Jewish worship, particularly their Sabbath keeping. So Christians felt compelled to divorce themselves completely from their Hebrew heritage. Although believers withstood outright idolatry—even to the point of death—pagan symbols and ceremonies slipped in the back door. Heathen holidays became Christian holy days.

Tell me. Have you ever wondered what Easter eggs and bunny rabbits have to do with the resurrection of Christ? Nothing, of course. They were pagan symbols of fertility. But the church adopted them to celebrate new life in Jesus. The *Encyclopedia Britannica* states, "Christianity . . . incorporated in its celebration of the great Christian feast day [Easter] many of the heathen rites and customs of the Spring festival."

Other heathen feasts besides Easter infiltrated the church. For centuries pagans celebrated the birth of their sun god Tammuz on December 25. Have you ever heard of that date?

Now there's nothing morally wrong with exchanging gifts at Christmas time—even if that isn't the true date of Christ's birth. Or hiding Easter eggs or putting bunnies in baskets for children. But here is my question. Since our Christian holidays originally came to us tainted with sun worship, how do we know that other areas of our worship, even truths morally vital, have not been tampered with too? Think about it.

So it was that Christians, seeking some relief from persecution, welcomed the rituals of sun worship. Of course, nobody suggests they actually worshiped the sun. They were simply celebrating Christ's birth and resurrection. So they reasoned.

Now this development did not happen in a corner. Scholars recognize these pagan roots in Christianity. No less an authority than Cardinal John Henry Newman tells the facts in his book *The Development of the Christian Religion:* "Temples, incense, oil lamps, votive offerings, holy water, holidays and seasons of devotion, processions, blessing of fields, sacerdotal vestments, the tonsure, and images . . . are all of pagan origin."— Page 359.

Now what do you think of that?

And, on the other hand, pagans actually became comfortable with Christianity. And why not? They could celebrate their heathen holidays in the name of Jesus. But a price had been paid. Pure faith lay buried deep in pagan tradition. Accommodation took the place of transformation. Diversion all too often replaced conversion.

By the fourth century, Christianity so resembled paganism that the emperor found it easy to become a believer. Constantine the Great proclaimed himself a convert in the year 312. Persecution ceased. Outright pagan sacrifices were outlawed. Christian worship became official. Delighted church leaders pledged to support the new Christian regime. Hand in hand, church and state mixed faith in Christ with sun-worship rituals. On March 7, 321, Constantine ordered his empire to reverence the "venerable day of the sun." Not the Son of God, you understand, but the sun. The day of pagan sun worship.

Sunday keeping by Christians was nothing new. Sometimes after Hadrian's second-century persecution of the Jews, the church in Rome had exchanged the Bible Sabbath for Sunday. So with Constantine's seal of approval, the day of the sun increased in importance to the church. In 538 a council at Orleans, France, forbade all work on the first day of the week. Eventually laws became so strict that a woman could be sentenced to seven days' penance for washing her hair on Sunday.

Sunday largely eclipsed the Sabbath in the western part of the empire, but in the east quite a few still worshiped on the seventh day. Many kept both days holy. Pockets of Sabbath keepers remained in areas known now as Egypt, Tunisia, Turkey, Palestine, and Syria. Also Ethiopia, Armenia, and Yugoslavia. Even in Ireland. Later—as late as the fifth century— evidence suggests that, Saint Patrick kept the seventh day holy.

Those who honored the Bible Sabbath found themselves in mortal danger. Anyone who accepted the Bible as the only rule of faith and who insisted upon Jesus alone as intercessor qualified as a heretic. The burning of heretics began at Orleans, France, in 1022. Persecution intensified during the great Crusades. Then came the infamous Inquisition, when the state enforced the teachings of the church. Thousands lost their lives for their simple faith in Christ.

These were dark ages for the church. How could Christians be so intolerant of their brothers and sisters in Christ? Jesus had predicted that those who killed His followers would sincerely think they were serving God. See John 16:2. Officials believed killing heretics saved thousands of others from following them into eternal torment. Even the heretics themselves might repent through fear of the flames. At least that's what many religious leaders hoped for.

It is not for us to question the motives of our medieval ancestors. Would it not be better to pray with our Saviour, "Father, forgive them, for they know not what they do"? Nor must we overlook the good done by the church. Throughout the world monasteries provided care for orphans, widows, and the sick. And all of us owe appreciation to the church of the Middle Ages for preserving the Scriptures.

Unfortunately, however, the Bibles were chained to monastery walls. Common people had to learn secondhand from the clergy. Knowledge of the Bible became scarce. Without question, the church was ripe for reform.

Should this erosion of Christian faith surprise us? After all, hadn't God's people in Old Testament times continually succumbed to false worship? The New Testament predicted that history would repeat itself. Apostasy would prevail in the church. The apostle Peter warned, "There will be false teachers among you, who will secretly bring in destructive heresies. . . . And many will follow their destructive ways." 2 Peter 2:1, 2.

Long ago, God's enemy learned a lesson. He had tried first to crush Christianity with persecution. It didn't work. So he resorted to deception. Quietly, gradually, he infiltrated the church with the trappings of sun worship. That *did* work.

Which do you think would be most deceptive today? Straightforward persecution? Or subtle infiltration—counterfeiting Christianity from within?

Today certain atheistic countries are waging open warfare against Christianity. Millions of persecuted believers stand brave and strong, while others forfeit their faith. But very few are deceived. It's easy to know what the enemy is up to when he threatens to throw you in jail for your faith.

Is the enemy using atheism now as a smoke screen? Is he diverting our attention as he undermines us with subtle change? Could it be that all the time we've been scouting the horizon for the antichrist, he has been growing in our own backyard?

Perhaps we ought to take another look at the meaning of the word *antichrist*. That could be our problem. *Anti*, means "against" or "instead of"—either to oppose Christ openly or to subtly overshadow Him. Which of these two types of warfare against Christ do we see in the antichrist?

In Thessalonians 2, verse 3 we read : "Let no one deceive you by any means; for that Day will not come unless the falling away comes first, and the man of sin is revealed, the son of perdition."

"Let no one deceive you," says the apostle. So deception is involved. No question about it. Evidently the antichrist results in a "falling away," a gradual apostasy within the body of believers. Didn't Jesus Himself warn about deception—about a wolf in sheep's clothing?

The antichrist. Dedicated men at different times reached the same conclusion. Martin Luther. John Knox, the Scottish Reformer. King James I, who commissioned our King James Bible. Sir Isaac Newton, the famous scientist and Bible student. Even the Puritan preacher John Cotton, known as the Patriarch of New England. Were they all mistaken? Or did they know something we've overlooked? And their conclusions you will not find in the many paperbacks professing to explain the antichrist which are found in the bookstores today.

So let's turn back to Revelation 13 and test the conclusions of the Reformers. You recall that the beast there has ten horns. Did the Roman empire collapse into these diverse kingdoms? Yes. The nations of modern Europe descended from them.

This beast has ten horns but only seven heads. How could this be? History explains. When the church took over the western empire, three tribes—the Heruli, the Vandals, and the Ostrogoths—rejected the popular Christian teachings and authority. So Emperor Justinian went to war on behalf of Christianity. The last of the rebels, the Ostrogoths, fell in the year 538. Ten kingdoms. And three of them fell. Just a coincidence? Or striking fulfillment of prophecy? Which?

Now what about the other attributes of antichrist? Let's read Revelation 13, beginning with verse 5: "He was given a mouth speaking great things and blasphemies, and he was given authority to continue for forty-two months. Then he opened his mouth in blasphemy against God, to blaspheme His name, His tabernacle, and those who dwell in heaven. And it was granted to him to make war with the saints and to overcome them." Verses 5-7.

Everything fits together so far. But what about these forty-two months? What time period do they represent? With thirty days to a lunar month, forty-two months would be 1260 days.

Are these literal or symbolic days? Remember, we are dealing with symbols here. Short-lived beasts symbolize centuries of government. So a much longer time span than 1260 literal days is called for.

Our perplexity vanishes when we understand that in symbolic prophecy, a day represents a year. Ezekiel 4:6 is one of several scriptures explaining the year/day principle. The Reformers suggested these 1260 days represent 1260 years of medieval Christian church-and-state authority, and history confirms it. After the Ostrogoths were defeated in 538, the church and state held power for this prophetic period, 1260 years, ending in 1798.

Long centuries of turmoil had finally come to an end. But now we want to know, What is next for Christianity? We'll find out in our next chapter, "Bloodstained Stars and Stripes." Here, however, is a one-paragraph preview.

We learned in this chapter that an unfortunate union of church and state took place in the early and middle centuries. This coalition, so clearly predicted in Scripture, played havoc with humanity's God-given freedom. But now Revelation reveals that an image, a likeness, a similar union will appear again down here in the end time of our world's history. It will be a union of many Christian groups uniting with the state, again acting out the character of antichrist in an attempt to coerce your conscience and mine.

Meanwhile, let's thank God for preserving His people through the ages. Although challenged by apostasy, many church fathers remained outstanding Christians. Like Augustine, a bishop in north Africa four centuries after Christ. His writings blessed God's people for centuries to come.

As a young man, Augustine had wandered from the faith of his childhood. But his dear mother never lost hope. Kneeling with an open Bible, she pleaded God's promises as only a mother can. Drawn at last through those faithful prayers, Augustine almost yielded to the Holy Spirit. Almost, but not quite. He begged the Lord, "Give me purity—but not yet." Have you ever prayed like that?

Finally he surrendered fully to the Lord Jesus Christ. Then he could pen that famous prayer so dear to Christians everywhere, "You have made us for Yourself, and our hearts will not find rest until they rest in You."

O friend, never forget. God made you for Himself. Your heart will never find rest until you rest yourself in Jesus. And you can do that right now.

Bloodstained Stars and Stripes

America is being born again! We've repented of the psyche-delic sixties and the secular seventies. Like reformed prodigals heading home, we're turning back to God.

Religion is even revolutionizing government. Lobbyists scurry about the halls of Congress with Bibles under their arms. One predicts, "If Christians unite, we can pass any law or any amendment. And that's exactly what we intend to do!"

Revival by legislation. What happens when faith is enforced by law? Will it lead to bloodstained Stars and Stripes?

Did you know that America's first settlers, Protestants and Catholics alike, suffered religious persecution? And, believe it or not, prophecy predicts intolerance will arise again in this fair land of ours. And sooner than we may think!

We come now to the seventh chapter in our study of the prophecies of Revelation. Here we will explore the mark of the beast. We will discover how God's enemy will replace religious zeal with incredible deceptions. And anyone who refuses to be deceived by his mysterious image will be persecuted.

We Americans prize our freedoms. It's easy to forget that liberty did not come naturally. Our early settlers fled their English homeland to escape persecution. Yet they often failed to open their own arms to other religious refugees.

When William Penn's band of Quakers sailed past the colony of Massachusetts, they nearly fell prey to a seventeenth-century inquisition. Listen to this order from Cotton Mather, the famous Puritan clergyman:

"There be now at sea a ship called 'Welcome,' which has on board 100 or more of the heretics and malignants called Quakers. . . . The General Court has given sacred orders to . . . waylay the said 'Welcome' . . . and make captive the said Penn and his ungodly crew, so that the Lord may be glorified and not mocked with the heathen worship of these people. . . . We shall not only do the Lord great good by punishing the wicked, but we shall make great good for His minister and people. Yours in the bowels of Christ, Cotton Mather."

Can you believe it! Thank God, the preacher's persecuting pirates failed. Penn's Quakers landed safely, and with their quiet faith to encourage them, they settled our great state of Pennsylvania.

The Puritans not only tyrannized others, they oppressed their own citizens. They arrested a sea captain and locked him in the stocks after he was caught kissing his wife on Sunday. One poor man fell into a pond and skipped Sunday services to dry his suit. They whipped him in the name of Jesus. John Lewis and Sarah Chapman, two lovers, were brought to justice for "sitting together on the Lord's day under an apple tree in Goodman Chapman's orchard."

Incredible legalism! And this in a land of freedom?

The Puritans with their Sunday laws tragically missed the meaning of Sabbath rest. They enforced a Sabbath of works on the first day of the week instead of the biblical seventh-day Sabbath. Understanding the freedom of Sabbath rest would have safeguarded the Puritans from persecuting—from forcing religion upon others.

Throughout Christian history, ignorance of Sabbath rest has invariably sparked persecution. The Pharisees plotted to destroy Jesus after a dispute about the Sabbath. See Mark 3:1-6. The rigid religion of that day led them to crucify the Lord of the Sabbath.

Overcome by legalism, the early Christian church finally abandoned the Sabbath. Sunday, a pagan day, displaced the seventh day. And those refusing to reverence this day of the sun were persecuted. The record of history is open for all to read.

Now come with me down to the Reformation of the sixteenth century. Earnest men of God called the church back to the Bible alone and salvation by faith alone. But many Protestants retained many of their medieval traditions. Like the Puritans, for example, with their Sunday laws. When Roger Williams arrived in Massachusetts in 1631, he protested their legislated legalism. Williams claimed civil magistrates had no right to enforce personal religion.

The colony condemned him in 1635. He escaped arrest and fled into the snowy forest, finding refuge with the Indians. He later commented, "I would rather live with Christian savages, than with savage Christians."

Roger Williams bought land from the Indians and established a new colony dedicated to religious liberty. He called his settlement Providence, today the capital of Rhode Island. Williams welcomed Jews, Catholics, and Quakers as citizens in full and regular standing.

Nobody suffered for their faith—or for refusing to believe. Sad to say, later leaders of Rhode Island lapsed into legalism and intolerance. And sure enough, they passed a Sunday law in 1679, requiring certain acts on Sunday and forbidding others.

Some of those early American Sunday laws packed a real sting. A Virginia law of 1610 provided that "those who violated the Sabbath or failed to attend church services, morning and afternoon, should on the first offense lose their provisions and allowance of the whole week following; for the second, lose their allowance and be publicly whipped; and for the third, suffer death."

Death for Sunday breaking! Keep that old Virginia law in mind when you hear it said that Sunday laws are a part of the great American heritage—and we must return to the "faith of our fathers."

While still a boy in Virginia, James Madison heard a fearless Baptist minister preaching from the window of his prison cell. That day Madison dedicated his life to fight for freedom of conscience. Tirelessly he toiled with Thomas Jefferson and others to secure the First Amendment in our Bill of Rights. It reads simply and majestically: "Congress shall make no law respecting an establishment of religion, or prohibiting the free exercise thereof." Government, you see, must protect religion—but not promote it.

Our founding fathers knew well the dangers of trying to cure unbelief by reverting to force. And so does God. Jesus put it plainly: "Render therefore to Caesar the things that are Caesar's, and to God the things that are God's." Matthew 22:21. Religious laws and civil laws then and now must be kept separate, or intolerance rears its ugly head.

Take, for example, this much-discussed matter of school prayer—a very live but delicate issue. I believe our children should lift their hearts in prayer everywhere, including in school. Especially in school! But who should teach our kids to pray? Do we want Protestant prayers? Catholic prayers? Jewish prayers? Does it matter? Not long ago the California state legislature selected a Buddhist chaplain. Would you like Buddhist prayers in your local school?

Who gets to choose what to pray? And who gets left out? Are you beginning to see the problems here?

Some say restoring prayer in our schools will solve our educational problems. I certainly believe in the power of prayer, but that may be going too far. I remind you that all these years prayer has opened every session of Congress. Has the opening legislative prayer balanced the national budget? Has it solved Capitol Hill's many problems?

Maybe legislated prayer isn't such a cure-all after all. And besides, could enforcing school prayer, as innocent and commendable as it seems, lead to other intrusions into private religion? Perhaps even intolerance again? It has happened before.

Long ago, God's Word predicted the religious freedom we enjoy in the United States. But prophecy also warns that we will lose that liberty. We read about it in Revelation 13:11: "I saw another beast coming up out of the earth, and he had two horns like a lamb and spoke like a dragon."

What is happening here? Remember that a beast in symbolic Bible prophecy represents a power—a kingdom—a nation. So after the dark ages of persecution another power emerges, fresh from the earth. Remember also that in our first chapter we identified this new nation as the United States.

In the Old World, church and state had formed a unit. But here we have a new form of government with two lamblike horns—the peaceful *separation* of the two powers of government and religion.

According to the prediction, evidently our lamblike nation will reverse its gentle manners and behave like a dragon. We'll go back to the Old World ways of the Puritans. Unfortunately, some unusual and distressing events will soon occur in America. Let's see verses 12-14:

"He exercises all the authority of the first beast in his presence, and causes the earth and those who dwell in it to worship the first beast, whose deadly wound was healed. He performs great signs, so that he even makes fire come down from heaven on the earth in the sight of men. And he deceives those who dwell on the earth by those signs which he was granted to do in the sight of the beast, telling those who dwell on the earth to make an image to the beast who was wounded by the sword and lived."

By miracles, counterfeit miracles, our nation will lead the world to form an image to the Old World beast. What could this mean? An image is a copy of the original. The Old World beast was a union of church and state, a religious system wedded to government and supported by law. This New World image to the beast, being a copy of this system, must also be a religious system united to government and supported by national law. How did the original beast gain power? Knowing this, we can understand the present-day image to the beast.

Back in the year 321, Emperor Constantine declared Sunday a national day of worship. That was the first recorded Sunday law. Eventually Christianity became the official state religion by order of Emperor Theodosius. And soon this all-powerful church-and-state combination of the Middle Ages began persecuting all who resisted its teachings.

I ask you, Is there any such religious movement today in America? Are we moving toward a marriage of church and state?

Americans are fed up. Fed up with the permissiveness and immorality of the sixties. Even yesterday's flower children have learned respect for law and order. Americans have also grown tired of the godless humanism of the seventies. We don't want atheistic concepts taught to our children. We want our public schools to promote prayer.

Now believe me, I fervently agree with these important moral reforms. But has the pendulum swung too far? Many believe that as long as government doesn't favor one particular church, all is well. To them, separation of church and state means there's no state-sponsored denomination. This sounds good. And it has been tried before here in America.

The colony of Maryland was founded primarily as a refuge for persecuted Catholics, but Christians of all faiths were welcomed. The Maryland assembly in 1649 proclaimed an Act of Toleration, which provided that all who confess Jesus shall be welcomed and tolerated.

Yet even this so-called Act of Toleration, as sincere as it was, inspired religious persecution. No liberty whatever was provided for non-Christians. And all who chose to disbelieve a particular doctrine of the Trinity were declared to be under the death penalty.

Persecution. It naturally results when faith becomes law.

Remember the march on Washington? Washington for Jesus? I was invited by the leader of nineteen respected television ministers—some of them personal friends—to join that march. But I had to decline. Why? There was so much about it that was good and commendable and desperately needed. Asking a nation to pray! What is wrong with that?

Very, very commendable, I say. But notice, it was not a march on Pittsburgh or a march on Los Angeles. It was a march on Washington. And it was to be held on the capitol steps between the houses of our law-making bodies, with some of these lawmakers present to give legislative backing.

I couldn't believe that Jesus, in whose honor the march was held, would be demonstrating if He were here. The government in His day was desperately corrupt and in need of reform. Yet He made no attempt to correct the evils that were so obvious.

Remember, He didn't reform that way. He never led a protest march. He was not a political activist. Rather, He knew that the problem lay deep in the hearts of mankind.

Did Jesus commission us, "Go, coerce all men"? Or "Go and teach"? Did He tell us to "tarry in Washington, until you get support from the government"? Did He say, "Ye shall receive power, after ye have gained control of the legislature"? Does Christ want us to depend upon His power, or on government?

Certainly I wish everybody would believe in God and live according to biblical morality. That's what "It Is Written" is all about. I have given my life for such convictions. We *ought* to be concerned and speak out candidly when we see our large cities guilty of the same sins that brought judgment upon ancient Sodom. But it is God who decided the fate of Sodom. I don't think we have been authorized to play God!

It would be a wonderful thing, I say, if everyone lived according to the Bible. But whose interpretation of the Bible? That is the question. You can see why I've always opposed any attempt to legislate personal morality. It has never worked. It didn't work with the Puritans, and it won't work now.

Never forget it, friend. Religious legislation is legalism. National salvation by works. Enforcing religion on weak human nature may produce the appearance of correct living. Outward conduct may be changed. But not the heart. No wonder Jesus said, "If you love me, keep my commandments." Speak out against the evils, yes—but attempt to legislate, no. Since God never forces faith, why should we?

Do you see now why the Bible offers a different solution for the spiritual problems of our land—the seventh-day Sabbath rest? Week by week the Sabbath invites our personal expression of faith—faith in God as our Creator and faith in God as our Redeemer. Had the Sabbath always been kept, there would be no atheism. No godless societies. Sincere Sabbath rest makes us moral without becoming legalistic. The other commandments put us to work. Only the Sabbath offers us rest in Christ. It provides a foundation of faith for the duties to God and neighbor outlined in the other nine commandments.

But many who don't understand Sabbath rest want to bring

back Sunday legislation to our modern society. They are urging Sunday laws in the name of social welfare. Requiring one day off is good for society, they say. Good for the family. Even good for saving energy. But don't believe it! Despite good intentions, Sunday laws have always brought persecution.

And the Revelation says that history will repeat itself. Is the image to the beast being formed now? Zealous Christians already want to enforce the morality of the majority. What will happen next? Let's go back to Revelation 13. Look at verses 16 and 17. We're reading here about the image to the beast in America.

"He causes all, both small and great, rich and poor, free and slave, to receive a mark on their right hand or on their foreheads, and that no one may buy or sell except one who has the mark or the name of the beast, or the number of his name."

Here we have an international boycott resulting in the mark of the beast, enforced by the image to the beast. Before we explore some clues as to what the mark might be, remember God's seal, His memorial of creation? Understanding God's seal helps us identify the contrasting mark.

In warning us to avoid that mark, the Bible commands us to worship Him who made heaven and earth. See Revelation 14:6, 7. So God's creatorship is a key issue in the final conflict. What memorial of creation has He given us? Could it be that God will use Sabbath rest to measure the loyalty of everyone who chooses to worship Him? I'm simply asking questions.

If Sabbath rest in Jesus represents God's seal, can we see what the mark might be? The Bible says, "They have no rest day or night, who worship the beast and his image." Revelation 14:11. No rest—no Sabbath rest!

Now I know the matter of God's day of rest may seem trivial. But really, the Sabbath controversy isn't between one day or another. Remember when former Soviet leader Khrushchev visited America? When he took off his shoe and pounded it on the speaker's platform? Suppose he had demanded that we Americans abandon our Fourth of July holiday and celebrate Independence Day on the fifth of July instead? Would Khrushchev have had the right to change our day? And suppose we had accepted his new day? What would that say about our loyalty to America?

The Sabbath controversy, I say, isn't over a day at all. It's over leadership. Will we obey our God—or yield to another god? Whom will we trust? Where is our loyalty? The worldwide test is coming soon.

No one has the mark of the beast today. Let me repeat that statement. No one has the mark of the beast today. God will not permit anyone to receive that mark until the issues are out in the open. But when the issues are fully explained, and all have had opportunity to understand and see the critical and final nature of the matter—then, if we deliberately choose to obey a command of men in place of a command of God, if we yield to coercion and take the easy way out—we will have marked ourselves, by our actions, as no longer loyal to God.

It's difficult to see how Bible believers could ever turn to force and coercion. But then, we must remember the Puritans.

Who knows what would happen to our freedom if we faced a national crisis? History reveals that people would willingly exchange their liberties for personal security. Is it possible that the majority will exchange some of their freedoms for the sake of economic and military security in an emergency?

The safety zone between church and state has been shrinking. The pendulum has swung so far to the right that we hear increasing talk of legislating morality. One Protestant leader recently declared on the CBS Evening News that "this notion of the separation of church and state was the figment of some infidel's imagination." Imagine!

More and more, in harmony with Revelation 13, we see attempts to erode our freedoms. And whenever the power of the state has enforced the goals of the church, personal liberty has been forfeited. Persecution has followed. Remember those old American Sunday laws?

Now I feel sure of this—when liberty is lost in this country it won't be because Americans have suddenly become cruel and bigoted. Rather, I'm convinced that our freedoms will be voted away, legislated away, amended away by well-meaning Christians who do not realize what they are doing. They will sacrifice our liberties in an attempt to solve our national problems, in a backlash against decades of permissiveness. In a reaction against shrinking morality, in the belief that a return to lost values is our only hope of regaining God's favor—they will discover too late that they have forged shackles for the soul.

Racing toward the crisis hour, we cannot ignore or escape the issues at stake. And our decision must be our own. Satan would like to force his way in. Sometimes even loved ones want to enter—loved ones who do not understand. But God Himself won't violate our freedom to choose. He stands at the door of our hearts and knocks. He waits for us to accept His love. Even though it may cost us our lives.

I think of that winter night when the Roman legion was encamped by a lake in Armenia. Several versions of the story exist. But evidently forty soldiers had refused to recant their faith. And they were sentenced to die out on the frozen lake. Banded together in the numbing cold, they began to sing. The stern, pagan commander, on watch from his comfortable tent, heard the words: "Forty wrestlers, wrestling for Thee, O Christ. Claim for Thee the victory and ask from Thee the crown."

Strangely moved, that hardened general, so used to cursing and frantic pleas for mercy, listened intently. These were men of his own company, men who had angered the authorities by their faith. These were his forty heroes, distinguished soldiers. Must they die?

He moved out into the cold, gathered driftwood from the shore, and built a huge fire with flames leaping high into the night. Perhaps this would lead them to renounce their faith and save themselves. But no. Again the sound of the refrain met his ears, weaker now: "Forty wrestlers, wrestling for Thee, O Christ."

Then suddenly, the song changed: "Thirty-nine wrestlers, wrestling for Thee, O Christ—"

And all at once, as the song still floated in across the ice, one of the prisoners climbed up the bank and dropped by the fire, a shivering mass. The song of the forty was no more. One of the heroes had disavowed his faith.

On the shore, clearly outlined against the fire, stood the commander. Strange thoughts surged in his heart. Suddenly he took one brief look at the pitiful traitor before him and threw off his cloak. Before his soldiers could stop him, he raced down the bank and across the ice to the freezing men, casting back the words, "As I live, I'll have your place."

In a few moments the song, with a fresh note of triumph, was wafted again to the soldiers who had gathered, fearful and awe-struck, on the silent shore: "Forty wrestlers, wrestling for Thee, O Christ, Claim for Thee the victory and ask from Thee the crown!"

God help us to awake—to see the vital issues at stake—and commit ourselves to the blessed Lord and Saviour Jesus Christ—quietly determined that we will be true to Him.

Airlift From Armageddon

Hiroshima, Japan. August 6, 1945. Morning dawned bright and clear with the promise of a beautiful day. Then suddenly at 8:16 it happened. And our world has never been the same.

"We have had our last chance," warned General Douglas MacArthur, several weeks after we dropped the bomb. "If we do not devise some greater and more equitable system [of settling international problems], Armageddon will be at our door."

Armageddon. The very word chills our spines. It's frightening! And it's almost upon us! But what really is Armageddon? Does anybody know?

If you consult popular religious paperbacks, you'll find some conflicting forecasts about Armageddon. You'll read about Russians pressing down from the north, Africans driving up from the south, Europeans and Americans swarming in from the west—and 200 million Chinese marching over from the east. All converging upon a battlefield in northern Israel. Does such a military nightmare lurk around the corner? Let's open the Bible and find out in the book of Revelation, chapter 16. This is the only place in all of God's Word where we read about Armageddon. Notice verses 14 and 16:

"They are the spirits of demons, performing signs, which go out to the kings of the earth and of the whole world, to gather them to the battle of that great day of God Almighty." "And they gathered them together to the place called in Hebrew, Armageddon."

So there will be an Armageddon. It's the final conflict of

earth's history, called "the battle of that great day of God Almighty." Apparently it's a global war, for the kings of the whole world are involved. And more than human forces will be fighting. The spiritual armies of God and Satan will clash in this battle. See Revelation 17:14.

Evidently Armageddon means much more than World War III. It represents an all-out showdown between God and His enemies—the climax of the great controversy between good and evil. The whole world will be involved in Armageddon—and heaven too!

Where will this battle be fought? Well, history offers no record of a place called Armageddon. But the Bible gives us some hints. Our text says the word *Armageddon* comes from the Hebrew language. Shall we turn to the Hebrew for the meaning of the word? We discover that it is a combination of *har*, which means mountain, and *mageddon*, which many connect with Megiddo. So the name Armegeddon can be understood as "mountain of Megiddo."

The mountain of Megiddo—here is a clue we can work with. Megiddo was a small but important fortress city of Old Testament times. It lay north of Jerusalem near the plain of Esdraelon. Once in Scripture this plain itself is called the plain of Megiddo. At first it might seem to be a logical location for warfare. But some problems make us pause and probe further.

First of all, the plain of Megiddo is rather small to host a global war. It's just two thirds the size of Lake Tahoe in northern California. Could you imagine the armies of the whole world, with millions of soldiers, in such crowded quarters? How would they all fit? And what about the armies of heaven? Remember also that Megiddo of Armageddon is neither a city nor a plain—it's a mountain. We must find a mountain of Megiddo. A mountain with some spiritual significance for the armies of heaven.

Visiting the site of ancient Megiddo, as I have done on a number of occasions, might help us understand Armageddon. We drive eastward from the Mediterranean port city of Haifa and follow the Carmel ridge. After passing the northeastern ridge of Carmel, we see the ruins of the ancient city. But also looming large over the landscape at Megiddo is Mount Carmel.

Maybe Mount Carmel solves our dilemma. Does it represent Mount Megiddo, the scene of Armageddon? Did something happen at Carmel that could help us understand Armageddon? Long ago Mount Carmel hosted a dramatic showdown between God and His enemies. The prophet Elijah summoned the nation to appear on the mountain. He challenged them to judge between Baal, the sun god, and the true God of heaven: "How long will you falter between two opinions? If the Lord is God, follow Him; but if Baal, then follow him." 1 Kings 18:21.

God won a great victory that day at Carmel. The nation declared allegiance to Him rather than to Baal. With one mighty voice they proclaimed, "The Lord, He is God! The Lord, He is God!" Verse 39. Following their vote of confidence in God and His government, they punished the false prophets who had led God's people astray.

So the call to Mount Carmel meant judgment—evaluating God and His government. And then a judgment of those who rejected Him. Should we expect some similar type of judgment in connection with Armageddon? What does the Bible say? Scripture reveals that Armageddon will occur during the seven plagues at the close of earth's history. Let's learn more about these plagues. God has been so patient all these years, sending sunshine and rain upon the good and evil alike. Now suddenly He sends wrath instead of rain. Why?

Let's go to Revelation 11. Has some type of judgment taken place in heaven? Has a verdict been reached? Let's read, beginning with verse 15: "Then the seventh angel sounded: And there were loud voices in heaven, saying, 'The kingdoms of this world have become the kingdoms of our Lord and of His Christ, and He shall reign forever and ever!' And the twenty-four elders who sat before God on their thrones fell on their faces and worshiped God, saying: 'We give You thanks, O Lord God Almighty, the One who is and who was and who is to come, because You have taken Your great power and reigned. The nations were angry, and Your wrath has come, and the time of the dead, that they should be judged, and that You should reward Your servants the prophets and the saints, and those who fear

Your name, small and great, and should destroy those who destroy the earth.' " Verses 15-18.

A remarkable scenario. What's happening here? A time to be judged, the text tells us. A judgment up in heaven while life continues here on earth. Just as at Carmel, God's government must be vindicated before He assumes His authority to punish the wicked. What's the purpose of this judgment? God cares about His reputation. He knows loyalty depends upon trust. So He determines to prove Himself trustworthy, allowing Himself to be audited. This same type of judgment occurs in the business world today. A corporation president, charged with dishonesty, may decide to open the books so every employee can see he has been just and fair. He wants to be trusted.

Now suppose he hasn't been honest in his dealings. Then he'll do everything possible to prevent such an audit. But God has nothing to hide. He invites inspection of His government. The apostle Paul understood this judgment when he wrote, "Let God be found true, though every man be found a liar, as it is written, 'That Thou mightest be justified in Thy words, and mightest prevail when Thou art judged.' " Romans 3:4, NASB.

So God will prevail when He is judged. Just as He won His case at Mount Carmel. God convinces His creation He is worthy of their worship. Satan's challenge is defeated at Armageddon. The kingdoms of this world become God's beyond dispute. Citizens of the universe stand behind Him as He rewards His people and punishes rebellion with the seven last plagues.

Is this judgment portrayed in the book of Revelation? Come with me to chapter 5. In Revelation 4 and 5, the apostle John describes what many consider to be the actual judgment scene in heaven's temple. Angels—myriads of them—gather to weigh the evidence. The evidence about God and His followers on earth. Scrolls, old-fashioned books, are opened.

Now, what's happening in the courts of heaven? Let's notice Revelation 5, verses 2, 3.

"I saw a strong angel proclaiming with a loud voice, 'Who is worthy to open the scroll and to loose its seals?' And no one in heaven or on the earth or under the earth was able to open the scroll, or to look at it."

Who is worthy? This is the crucial question. John watches with interest to see who will pass the judgment. But no one is worthy. No one in heaven. No one on the earth measures up to the scrutiny of judgment. Not even John himself, a disciple of Jesus. And no one under the earth—no one in the grave—is worthy,

John begins to "weep greatly." (NASB) Is this disappointed curiosity? No, much more than that. He's worried about the judgment. If nobody can survive the scrutiny of heaven's court, what hope does he have? Everyone is unworthy. Everyone, that is, but Jesus. See verse 5:

"One of the elders said to me, 'Do not weep. Behold, the Lion of the tribe of Judah, the Root of David, has prevailed to open the scroll and to loose its seven seals.' "

What comfort for our hearts—the Lord Jesus Christ is declared worthy! He prevails in heaven's court. And when our Saviour wins the verdict, we win too, for our lives belong to Him. We overcome in the blood of the Lamb.

Remember the story of those plagues in Egypt? What saved God's people from the death angel? Blood on their doorposts. God promised, "When I see the blood, I will pass over you; and the plague shall not be on you to destroy you when I strike the land of Egypt." Exodus 12:13.

The blood, friend—that's what counts! The blood of Jesus. We're safe from the plagues in our Saviour's blood. When every soul decides for life or death, earth's harvest will be ripe. All who trust in Jesus are sealed for eternal life. And those who refuse God's salvation will lose their lives.

You may remember hearing about Harry Truman. I don't mean the former president. This was the Harry Truman who owned the Mount Saint Helens Lodge in the state of Washington. Those who lived near the volcanic mountain had been warned about an imminent eruption. But some of them, including eighty-four-year-old Harry, refused all attempts to save them from their beloved mountain.

Harry told his would-be rescuers, "There's nothing that mountain could do to scare me off." Saint Helens, you see, was like a friend to him. He felt safe, having lived there for fifty-four years. He even boasted, "No one knows more about this mountain than Harry, and it don't dare blow up on him."

But it did. It happened the morning of May 18, 1980. An explosion twenty-five hundred times more powerful than the blast that ripped Hiroshima came as an overwhelming surprise. Today poor Harry and dozens of others lie buried beneath the volcanic mud. They gambled their lives with the mountain—and lost. They had been warned, but they refused to be saved. Why is it we find it so hard to heed warnings?

Just before the destruction of this world, God sends three angels with special urgent worldwide warnings. We find them in Revelation 14. Each angel proclaims a segment of the message that is God's last communication to the human race. Of course, these angels are symbolic. They are not flying over our heads with a megaphone. We find the first warning in Revelation 14:6, 7:

"I saw another angel flying in the midst of heaven, having the everlasting gospel to preach to those who dwell on the earth—to every nation, tribe, tongue, and people—saying with a loud voice, 'Fear God and give glory to Him, for the hour of His judgment has come; and worship Him who made heaven and earth, the sea and springs of water.' "

Here's the everlasting gospel, the grand old message of salvation. But now with a new urgency. Why? Because "the hour of His judgment has come." A judgment like that at Mount Carmel of long ago.

Next comes the second angel, warning about false worship. Then finally the third angel, sounding the alarm about the mark of the beast. So every soul decides for life and death. Those faithful to God receive His seal. The disobedient receive the mark of the beast and the plagues. After the seventh and last plague, Christ returns to airlift His people from Armageddon. We will rise through the sky to our heavenly home. And what a homecoming that will be!

Remember the day our hostages came home from Iran? The long ordeal ended almost as suddenly as it had begun. The fear and the hunger, the blindfolds and the isolation and the beatings, the terrible loneliness, the fake firing squads—all slipped into the past. Four hundred and forty-four dull, dragging, seemingly endless days suddenly gave way to a tumult of joy and reunion. A welcome that couldn't happen except in a dream. Yet it was happening—happening to fifty-two Americans who in their darkest hours had been tempted to think they had been forgotten.

It would take a while to sort it all out and be convinced that it was real! Telephones! Milk to drink! No blindfolds! Moving about without asking permission! German children singing to make up for the Christmases they had missed. The Statue of Liberty lighted for the first time since 1976! Kissing American soil! Church bells ringing! Falling at last into the arms of loved ones! The memories were theirs to keep.

And each day brought more pictures to hang in memory's hall. Pictures framed by bus windows as they inched through the cheering crowds. The Lincoln Memorial bathed in colored lights. The President praying simply, "Dear God, thank You! Thank You for what You've done!"

Americans had not been content simply to tie yellow ribbons 'round old oak trees. They tied them everywhere. On trees. On cars. On planes. On gates. On buildings. They tied one completely around the National Geographic Building. And the biggest yellow ribbon in history was tied in a bow around the Superdome in New Orleans!

Miles and miles of ribbons—beside the highways and above them. Corridors of welcome the freed hostages would never forget! Americans watched it all—from the streets and from their living rooms—and wept for joy. The hostages were safe! They were free! Home at last—and how happy we were to have them back!

What a celebration! Just like that unforgettable day in France at the end of World War I. As twenty thousand soldiers approached the Arc de Triomphe, a great choir sang the joyful challenge, "By what right do you come to the arch of victory?" Can you imagine the inspiration and emotion when 20,000 voices responded, "We come by the blood-red banner of Verdun!"

Soon the Lord Jesus Christ will sweep through the gates of

heaven with the redeemed of all the ages. I can imagine the angel choir greeting us with the challenge, "By what right do you enter here?" And we will unite in the mighty chorus, "We come by the blood-red banner of Calvary!" What a day that will be! Please don't miss it!

After the homecoming celebration, we will settle down to enjoy eternity with our Lord and Saviour. Listen to this description of our paradise home. It's taken from *The Great Controversy,* one of my favorite books.

"There are ever-flowing streams, clear as crystal, and beside them waving trees cast their shadows upon the paths prepared for the ransomed of the Lord. There the wide-spreading plains swell into hills of beauty, and the mountains of God rear their lofty summits. On those peaceful plains, beside those living streams, God's people, so long pilgrims and wanderers, shall find a home."

"The great controversy is ended. Sin and sinners are no more. The entire universe is clean. One pulse of harmony and gladness beats through the vast creation. From Him who created all, flow life and light and gladness, throughout the realms of illimitable space. From the minutest atom to the greatest world, all things, animate and inanimate, in their unshadowed beauty and perfect joy, declare that God is love."—Pages 675, 678.

O friend, can you picture it? All things new! Just as they were at creation. Won't it be wonderful when Jesus comes? And I believe He is coming soon! God help us to join with the apostle, responding, "Even so, come, Lord Jesus!"

And now as we close this series on Revelation, my prayer for you is found in the very last verse of the book: "The grace of our Lord be with you all. Amen." Revelation 22:21.

Fifteen Minutes More

It was the gay century of knights and queens. Queen Elizabeth and her favorite escort, the Earl of Leicester. The year—1575.

It was Lord Leicester's desire that the queen visit his proud Kenilworth Castle in the Midlands of the British Isles. She accepted the invitation. Extravagant plans for the celebration were laid. The gardens were exotically trimmed and the castle elegantly decorated. Titled guests were to overflow its courts. Lord Leicester had lavished a fortune on pageantry that excited the whole countryside. Eleven-year-old Shakespeare might well have trudged the thirteen miles from neighboring Stratford-on-Avon to mingle with the curious spectators.

But on the eve of the visit, Lord Leicester called his servants together for one final word of instruction: "On the morrow, when the queen steps across the threshold, I ask that the great clock be stopped, never to be started again."

The morning dawned bright and clear. At the appointed hour, the queen's courtiers appeared, the drawbridge was lowered, trumpets blew loud and long. And then, as the queen of England stepped across the threshold into the castle, the great timepiece was stopped, forever marking the historic moment of the queen's arrival.

Talking about clocks—stopped clocks. Time for this sophisticated generation is running out. The ominous swinging of the pendulum is forcing from thousands of frightened lips the frantic cry, "*Oh, God, give us fifteen minutes more, please!*"

However graphic the story of Queen Elizabeth's visit, it is but an inadequate illustration of an hour soon to strike when another monarch will step across the threshold—this time the threshold of a world.

At that hour every clock, every watch, every timepiece the world around, will be forever stopped, never to be started again. For at that moment, when the Saviour of our world steps across its threshold as King of kings and Lord of lords, time will melt into eternity.

Watch with me as earth's clock ticks its last moments into history—about to be stopped by God Himself.

For centuries, the Christian church has taught that Jesus would return to this world a second time, and that His coming would bring an end to our world, as we know it, to make way for a better one. All sober thinking these days takes into account such a possibility. Some may not like it, may not care to adjust to it, but none dare ignore it.

The man on the street is more bewildered, more apprehensive, more insecure than ever before. He senses that something—some event of world magnitude—is about to take place. But he says, "How can I know *when* it will happen and how it will affect me?"

A reasonable question. But you see, in the predictions of scripture God clearly outlines the future. He warns the rebellious of a day when once again He will personally intervene in human history. He promises His people a day of grand fulfillment. And He permits us a glimpse of His timepiece, permits us to watch the hands of His clock as we witness the speeding events of our time.

In the sacred pages of Scripture, you will discover not only awareness of the hour, but also confidence to meet it. For aside from the forgiving grace of God, nothing, absolutely nothing, will bring you more peace, more security than the simple, straightforward, unequivocal promise of Jesus, "I will come again."

"Let not your heart be troubled: ye believe in God, believe also in me. In my Father's house are many mansions: if it were not so, I would have told you. I go to prepare a place for you.

And if I go and prepare a place for you, I will come again, and receive you unto myself, that where I am, there ye may be also." John 14:1-3, KJV.

If words have meaning, is there any possibility of misunderstanding our Lord's promise?

"But," comes the question, "when will it take place?"

Did you know that the disciples asked that very question?

"Tell us, when shall these things be? and what shall be the sign of thy coming, and of the end of the world?" Matthew 24:3, KJV.

In answer, our Lord made it very clear that while we *cannot* know the day or the hour of His coming, yet graphic signs of our times *will* reveal the nearness of that event. We find His answer in this same twenty-fourth chapter of Matthew. Listen:

"Ye shall hear of wars." Matthew 24:6, KJV.

"Nation shall rise against nation." Matthew 24:3, KJV.

Has not this last generation seen more of war at its worst—more fighting on a global scale, with more destructive forces and more serious worldwide complications—than all previous generations combined?

The malady of war, contained in one spot, breaks out in another. We talk peace—but we go on counting our missles. Nuclear war did not seem quite such a threat so long as we alone possessed its secret. But now nation after nation has joined the nuclear club. Dictators flex their muscles in megatons. And this planet trembles for its life!

"There shall be famines." Matthew 24:7, KJV.

"Earthquakes in many places." Matthew 24:7, NEB.

Famines? Economists tell us that we are only a little way from global famine. And when the contagion of want invades the privileged nations, then who will feed the world?

Earthquakes? This old world is convulsing at nature's depths. It is estimated that there are approximately a million earthquakes annually.

Did you know that the Alaska upheaval of 1964 tore the earth's surface worse than any previous recorded tremor? Energy released during the quake and its aftershocks was equal to 500,000 times the power of the nuclear bomb dropped on Hiroshima. Mercifully, most of the quake's force was expended beneath the ocean. But what would happen if a force equal to 500,000 nuclear bombs should strike a thickly populated area such as Los Angeles or Tokyo?

"Earthquakes in many places," said Jesus. And we watch the subtle, unobtrusive slipping of the faults in the earth—and try to guess where next, and when.

"False prophets will arise." Matthew 24:24, RSV.

No generation has been more inclined to probe the future than our own. Best sellers and mystics and crystal balls compete for the spotlight. Are they true prophets—or false? How do they measure up?

One widely consulted prophetess, asked on television if her predictions agreed with those of Scripture, replied in surprise, "I don't know! No one has ever asked me that before!"

Wouldn't you think it vitally important to find out?

"Because of the increasing crime wave, most people's love will grow cold." Matthew 24:12, Williams.

Need I comment? Has any other generation produced more brazen assassins than ours? Shooting at random from the top of the Texas Tower. The mass murder of eight nurses. Men, women, and children slaughtering their own families. Women strangled in uncanny succession. Hearts so calloused that a son could phone his mother-in-law and announce, "I'm shooting your daughter right now!" And three shots rang into the ears of a helpless mother hundreds of miles away as she listened to the dying screams of her daughter.

Jesus said it would be like the days of Noah.

"As were the days of Noah, so will be the coming of the Son of man." Matthew 24:37, RSV.

Noah's generation was a permissive generation. So is ours. So permissive that fathers and mothers, in too many homes, have lost not only their halos but their authority. This is the day of abandoned moral codes, of situation ethics, and the new morality—with all the frustrating results.

Remember the days when a boy who accidentally broke a neighbor's window had to pay for it out of his allowance? But what about the 200 students, protesting the make-up of a faculty committee, who occupied the university's ninth-floor computer center? When the committee make-up remained unchanged, they took axes and hacked the computers to bits—$1,600,000 worth. Their punishment? You guess.

But now listen to the description of the last days in the book of Daniel, prime minister-prophet of Babylon:

"But thou, O Daniel, shut up the words, and seal the book, even to the time of the end: many shall run to and fro, and knowledge shall be increased." Daniel 12:4, KJV.

Notice. The time of the end is to be marked by two distinctive features unparalleled anywhere else in history—increase of knowledge, and speed of travel.

Primarily, of course, this refers to an increase in the understanding of the Word of God. But it is also true that our generation has seen more increase of knowledge in general, and more acceleration in speed, than all other generations in history combined. I don't think anyone will challenge that statement.

For thousands of years men have lived and loved. They have fought and died. But only in our day have telephones and railroads, radio and television and radar, electronics and jet propulsion, become a part of everyday living. We are now planning computers that will zip ahead of our thoughts in billionths of a second. We talk casually of supersonics and ultrasonics, of flying discs and jet-propelled craft that defy the very laws that have governed man for centuries. We are not far from a global communications network of satellites.

Air traffic jams, delays and diversions, are the order of the day. Planes waiting to land in Chicago are stacked up into Nebraska. The shortage of trained control personnel is frightening. Airports have had to face the staggering task of converting their facilities to handle the jumbo jets and the supersonic transports.

Spacecraft that travel 25,000 miles an hour are an everyday thing. We orbit the moon on Christmas Eve. And then, three flights later, we move on to land on its surface, leaving our boot marks on its powdery terrain, and littering the moonscape with our paraphernalia.

The mind can scarcely comprehend the exactness with which

our space scientists make their calculations. For instance, lift-off for *Apollo XI* was late, they say—late by 724 milliseconds! And when Neil Armstrong called back from Tranquillity Base, "The Eagle has landed," it was only 90 seconds earlier than the landing time scheduled months before. Such precision—on such an untried mission—is incredible!

What did Daniel tell us? Knowledge shall be increased?

And what shall we say of the yet hidden secrets of the next war that frighten our imagination? Already submarines circle the globe powered by a handful of uranium. We have made missiles that cannot miss. And think of it! Computer warfare! Tanks that will not carry cannons or rocket launchers, but high-powered lasers that can vaporize any material—even steel or diamonds! Thermonuclear insanity!

Says J. Robert Moskin, writing in a popular magazine, "Scientists . . . forsee a fascinating array of new toys for the soldiers: disintegrator ray guns; acoustic shock waves; cheap, lightweight nuclear weapons that even gangsters can make; ocean-bed fortifications; and anti-gravity mechanisms that will give future GI's three-dimensional mobility. They even expect weather wars, with one side stirring up hurricanes to wreak havoc on the other. But warfare may become less gory with the development of non-lethal gases, and with battles fought 20,000 feet under the sea or between unmanned satellites in outer space."

For a moment of almost ridiculous contrast, may I remind you that about a century ago an employee of the United States Patent Office resigned his position. The reason? Everything that could be invented, had been invented, he said. He felt it was only wise to anticipate the day when he would be asked to find other employment. And that, friend, was before the great mass of present-day inventions tumbled into an unsuspecting world.

Yes, a man was once considered insane because he declared that an engine could travel at the tremendous speed of 12 miles an hour. Today we build metroliners with a speed that sucks the windows out of the trains they pass!

Have you ever wondered why all this increase of knowledge

was not spread out a little more evenly over world history? Why did not some of it come in Abraham's day, or those of the Caesars? Modes of travel in the days of our grandparents were little different from those used in the days of Abraham.

To be sure, the schedule of Bible prediction places this increase of knowledge in the last end of history. But why? Is there not a reason why it could not be otherwise? I believe there is.

What is man doing with this knowledge? Are not his ingenious devices, the keenness of his brain, actually unlocking secrets of the universe which he is morally incapable of handling? Is not man's knowledge aimed at his own destruction?

Do you wonder that God did not permit all this two thousand years ago? Might not man have blown the world to bits before the Saviour could have died for you and me?

How can I escape this conviction? The very fact that God has permitted men to unlock the secrets of the universe is one conclusive proof that He must be about to step across the threshold of time to bring an end to this world as we know it. The God of heaven could not take such a risk except in such an hour—an hour when He stands ready to intervene in the affairs of men.

Is there not but one explanation for it all? You and I stand not only *near* the final hour, but *on the very verge of it!*

The words of the commentator Leland Stowe are more uncannily appropriate today than when he wrote them decades ago. Listen:

"We have telescoped a score of centuries. . . . At last there exists a universal time-fuse. . . . This is the jest to end all jesting. Why did we, who know so little, seek to pry earth's last and mightiest secret from her breast? But now it's done. . . . But our fingers and our hearts and minds are what they were before. . . . And measuring the desperateness of our task, we may well plead: *'Just fifteen minutes more, please!'* "

Yes, we are heading toward the day everything stops—so far as this world is concerned. Not because we have at last crowded ourselves off this planet. Not because we have managed to get ourselves into a massive air-land-and-sea traffic jam so enormous, so impossible that it brings life to a standstill. But because the Creator Himself comes down to this earth and says,

"It is enough! It's closing time!"

And at that moment earth's pendulum will shudder and stop in midswing!

This generation seems to sense its doom. It is afraid—so afraid that the rays of the rising moon, unrecognized on the radar screen, could send our defense forces into panic, if not into nuclear war. And the record shows that I'm not dreaming!

But Jesus said it would be this way: "And there shall be signs in the sun, and in the moon, and in the stars; and upon the earth distress of nations, with perplexity; . . . men's hearts failing them for fear, and for looking after those things which are coming on the earth. . . . And then shall they see the Son of man coming in a cloud with power and great glory." Luke 21:25-27, KJV.

"Distress of nations, with perplexity." And that word translated "perplexity" means literally "no way out." H. G. Wells said, "There is no way out, or round, or through the impasse. *It is the end!*"

It is this frustration of impossible situations that causes men's hearts to fail for genuine fear of what they see coming upon the earth.

And the only solution to the fear, the stark fear that men face today, is the voice that comes down to us from the Mount of Olives. That voice, friend, is far more dependable, infinitely more assuring, than that of any statesman, any lawmaker, any human authority on world affairs.

The Christ of Bethlehem's manger, the Man of Calvary, quietly ascending from the Mount of Olives, left His faithful followers to find not only comfort but assurance in the parting words of the angel: "This same Jesus, which is taken up from you into heaven, shall so come in like manner as ye have seen him go into heaven." Acts 1:11, KJV.

Christ is the answer, friend—Christ and His return to earth. Christ is the way out where there seems to be no way out. I have no plan of my own, no utopian dream, no human panacea. But I offer you the simple promise of the Saviour, "I will come again."

A young stranger to the Alps was making his first climb, accompanied by two stalwart guides. It was a steep, hazardous ascent. But he felt secure with one guide ahead and one following. For hours they climbed. And now, breathless, they reached for those rocks protruding through the snow above them—the summit.

The guide ahead wished to let the stranger have the first glorious view of heaven and earth, and moved aside to let him pass. Forgetting the gales that would blow across those summit rocks, the young man leaped to his feet. But the chief guide dragged him down. "To your knees, sir!" he shouted. "You are never safe here except on your knees!"

Yes, friend, to your knees! No other position is safe in this hour. The summit rocks are just ahead. We hear the roaring of the gales. It is an hour for prayer.

Showdown in the Middle East

Once upon a time, according to the legend, a scorpion came to the Jordan River and wanted to get across. But he couldn't swim. He saw a frog there on the shore, and he said, "Dear frog, would you kindly carry me across the river?"

But the frog dived into the river as he said, "I wouldn't dream of it. I know you. You might sting me."

"Oh, no," said the scorpion, "have no fear. If I did that while we were crossing the river, then we would both perish."

That reassured the frog. So he came back to shore and said, "Hop on my back, then, and I will give you a ride across."

So the scorpion hopped on the frog's back and they started across. But in midstream the scorpion suddenly stung the frog. As the two were sinking beneath the waves, the frog cried out, "Scorpion, why did you do that? Now we shall both die!"

And the scorpion replied, "Well, this is the Middle East!"

Yes, that's the Middle East. Confused. Puzzling. Explosive. Unreasonable. It's a land of changing alliances where the frog today may be the scorpion tomorrow. Ready to sting at the slightest provocation. Even if the whole Middle East should sink!

Such is the strange reasoning—or lack of reasoning—in that part of the world. And it is no secret that the peace and security of the whole planet it tied to what happens in the Middle East.

Why is this? Why will a great superpower wink at aggression in some other part of the world, but bristle with threats at the slightest approach toward the Persian Gulf?

What do these mysterious lands have that others so desperately want? Oil. It wouldn't take much of a prophet to predict that a military showdown in the Middle East would be over oil.

Complicating the problem, and greatly increasing its explosiveness, is the fact that the conflict, more and more, has taken on religious overtones. A secular power will coldly calculate the cost of its moves. But when people's first loyalty is to religion, there may be no calculation at all.

It was bad enough when Arabs claimed lands as their homes because they had lived there for thousands of years and Israelis claimed the same lands because God gave them to their ancestors in the days of Abraham.

But how could you deal with a people that didn't mind being stung by the scorpion, that didn't mind sinking, that wouldn't mind dying in "serving God"? What does a nation of would-be martyrs care about international law, world opinion, or military threats?

On the other hand, would it help if we better understood the world of Islam, the background and perspective from which the Muslim views the West?

The forces of an Islamic revival, which dominated the news in the late seventies, seemed to Westerners like the return of medieval barbarity. No wonder news commentators could not understand the closing of bars, casinos, and cinemas, and the execution of prostitutes and other moral offenders.

But conservative Christians should have understood. For they frown upon many of the same sins. Yet, they do not deal with offenders so harshly. Flogging a criminal for some petty offense, amputating a hand for theft, or shooting a girl for immoral conduct seems far too severe.

But the truth is that the permissiveness of the West, the failure of Christianity to live up to its own moral standards, is a big part of the problem. The Muslim often feels vastly superior to the Christian. After all, why should America tell a Muslim country what to do—when American Christians worship "three gods," bow to idols, and frequently get drunk?

Let me illustrate. An Australian couple stopped over in an Arab city. They approached a local businessman in the lobby of the hotel and asked where they might see a belly dance. The businessman frowned and looked them over carefully. He noticed the woman wore no wedding ring. Obviously, to him, they were simply immoral Europeans out to enjoy the worst of life.

So what did the businessman do? Motivated by both honor and hospitality, he invited the couple to dinner with his family in a good restaurant. In that way he helped the Australians to avoid such evils as dance shows.

Another instance. A man approached a fruit vendor selling melons from a cart. He found an overripe Crenshaw melon that smelled delicious and wanted to buy it. It had a bruised spot, however. You would expect the fruit vendor to be delighted to get rid of a melon that would soon rot. Instead, he absolutely refused to sell it, and finally threw it on the ground.

A few minutes later, as he wandered on through the marketplace, this same man felt a tap on his shoulder, and half a cucumber was thrust into his bag. A merchant had charged him too much for some cucumbers and was correcting his mistake.

Said a devout Muslim who had been reading *Newsweek* magazine, with its recital of crime and corruption, "I don't understand why you Americans send all these missionaries over here!"

Perhaps now we can understand just a little better the label "Satan America."

But understanding does not make the Middle East less explosive. Nor does it make its problems easier to untangle. The whole area sits upon a pool of oil. And no one knows which fuse will ignite it first!

When we turn to the area of Bible prophecy, particularly prophecies about Israel, a great deal of confusion still exists. There are sincere Bible students who have constructed from Scripture a series of end-time events that they believe are about to take place in Israel, centering in Jerusalem and including the building of another temple. They are carefully watching events in Israel, and estimating the nearness of our Lord's return accordingly.

The problem is that there are many, many Bible predictions about Israel. But many of them were conditional upon what ancient Israel did or did not do. Many of the promises clearly contain an "if." *If* the people were loyal to God, *if* they remained faithful to Him, He would do certain things for them.

But when Israel as a nation failed to carry out its appointed mission as a light to the world, when it forfeited its position as a chosen people by the rejection of Christ as the Messiah, a change in relationship came in. The promises made to Israel on the condition of obedience could not be fulfilled to them. They would now be reserved for spiritual Israel, for Jews and Gentiles alike who have accepted Christ. And most of these promises will find fulfillment only in the future life, in the earth made new.

One of the reasons that Jesus was rejected by His own people is that the religious leaders of His day had misapplied Scripture. They had taken scriptures that apply to our Lord's second coming in glory and forcibly applied them to their own time. Then they rejected Jesus because He did not fit their mistaken assumptions, because He did not come as a King.

That same sort of thing may happen today. There is danger that we should become so engrossed with our assumptions about Jerusalem—which likely are mistaken assumptions— that we are completely surprised, taken unaware, by the return of our Lord in the skies!

This, however, is not to deny that the Middle East, from the beginning, has been the focal point of the history of this planet. I wonder if you realize that almost every great event, so far as the relation of this planet to its God is concerned, has centered, or will center, in the Middle East. And every major confrontation between God and His enemies, every major showdown, has been in that part of the world. The final showdown just ahead of us, though it will involve the whole planet, will still have a focal point in the Middle East.

There is no way that we can know the location of Eden, the garden home that the Creator prepared for our first parents. The book of Genesis tells us that a river flowed out from Eden and divided into four. The names of two of these rivers, the Tigris and the Euphrates, have caused some to speculate that the Garden of Eden was in the Mesopotamian Valley. However, the entire surface of the planet was so drastically altered at the time of Noah's Flood that it is impossible to tie any post-Flood locality to pre-Flood days.

After the Flood, however, we are not left to speculation. We are told definitely that the ark came to rest "upon the mountains of Ararat." Genesis 8:4.

It is no surprise, then, that recorded history seems to radiate from that area.

Since those early days, many have been the enormously important political and religious showdowns centering in the explosive Middle East. In these pages we will focus on three. Perhaps the most important of all, Middle East showdowns.

Approximately 1500 years, B.C., along the banks of the Nile, a head-on confrontation took place between God and an Egyptian king who was as stubborn and as unpredictable as any ayatollah!

Then in the days of Elijah came a second showdown, with the prophet Elijah standing alone against 450 prophets of Baal, the sun-god. That is one of the most thrilling stories of all time.

The third major showdown is yet to come. We call it Armageddon. And already we can feel its fiery breath!

The first two confrontations happened in the Middle East. The third, Armageddon, will also have its focal point there.

Add to this the fact that Jesus, the Son of God, when He came to live among us, was born, lived, and was crucified in the Middle East. From there He ascended to heaven. When He returns to take His people to the home prepared for them, His coming will be witnessed worldwide (Revelation 1:7), and He will catch His people up into the cloud of angels without Himself touching the earth (1 Thessalonians 4:16, 17).

But when, after a thousand years (Revelation 20:4, last part), Jesus returns to this earth with His people, again the point of contact will be the Middle East. We are told that His feet will stand upon the Mount of Olives, just outside Jerusalem (Zechariah 14:4). The mountain will become a great plain on which the New Jerusalem, moved from heaven to earth (Revelation 21:2, 10), will rest. And it is there, outside the city, that rebellion will meet its final judgment and sin will be no more. Revelation 20:9.

Such is the story of the Middle East, from start to finish. It might even be called the navel of this planet, the point of attachment to its Creator.

The great confrontations between God and those who oppose His designated people are (which in these pages we shall view in more detail) all a part of a great controversy that began in heaven. It began when heaven's highest angel challenged the government of God, in particular the authority of Christ. Lucifer, that exalted angel, proud of his own beauty, had determined to gain for himself the place of Christ, the Son of God. "How art thou fallen from heaven, O Lucifer, son of the morning! how art thou cut down to the ground, which didst weaken the nations! For thou hast said in thine heart, I will ascend into heaven, I will exalt my throne above the stars of God: . . . I will ascend above the heights of the clouds; I will be like the most High." Isaiah 14:12-14, KJV.

The conflict, primarily, is between Christ and Lucifer, now called Satan. But it also involves the angels loyal to Christ and the angels who rebelled with Lucifer. For we read, "There was war in heaven: Michael [Christ] and his angels fought against the dragon; and the dragon fought and his angels, and prevailed not; neither was their place found any more in heaven. And the great dragon was cast out, that old serpent, called the Devil, and Satan, which deceiveth the whole world: he was cast out into the earth, and his angels were cast out with him." Revelation 12:7-9, KJV.

This planet, then, became the theater of conflict. And now every member of the human race is involved. We are involved because our first parents, by open disobedience, involved us.

It is important to remember, then, as the controversy winds up to its final climax, that the participants are still the same. The angels of God and the angels of Satan, though invisible to us, are still in conflict. Said the apostle Paul, "We wrestle not against flesh and blood, but against principalities, against powers, against the rulers of the darkness of this world, against spiritual wickedness in high places." Ephesians 6:12.

Only as we remember the nature of this conflict and who the participants are, only then will we be able to understand what is happening today. For the book of Revelation tells us clearly that Satan's angels, his angels-turned-demons, are stirring up the nations to an anger that will soon culminate in Armageddon.

We shall discover, as we look at these three great showdowns, some most striking parallels. In all three the issues are the same. All three are a challenge to God's authority. In all three there is an involvement with sun worship. Even in our day? Yes, even in our day. In all three there is an attack upon God's law. In all three the cherished objects of false worship are unmasked completely, shown to be incapable of saving their followers. And in all three a clear line is drawn between those who serve God and those who serve Him not.

In our day, in the eyes of many, it is coming to be considered something of a crime to discriminate between those who do right and those who do wrong. But God discriminates. He makes a clear distinction—so clear that no man can miss it!

And then, after looking closely at the three great showdowns, we shall discover that the life of Jesus, particularly as it led to the cross, was the greatest showdown of all. For Calvary was a head-on collision with the invisible forces of Satan. And it was Satan who lost!

Recently I heard of a man, a Cambodian I believe, who found a Bible. It was a Bible from which the first six chapters of Genesis and the last ten chapters of Revelation were missing. And I was thinking—that if the situation had been reversed, if he had *only* the first six chapters of Genesis and the last ten chapters of Revelation—he still could have discovered the way to Christ and to life. He still could look to the future with hope and confidence.

In the early pages he would have seen man created in the image of God, with limitless possibilities. And then the intrusion of an enemy. Man's tragic fall. But immediately the promise of a Saviour. Yet, in spite of that divine provision, the increase of rebellion—until God found it necessary to destroy almost the entire human race in a global flood.

Turning to the final chapters of Revelation, that man with his abbreviated Bible would see that the conflict is not over. He would see it accelerating to a fearful climax as the armies of men and of demons make war with the Lamb. But he sees the Lamb victorious. He sees a new heaven and a new earth—and an endless day where heartache and tears and sin and death itself are forever gone. And he is led to pray with John who wrote the book, "Even so, come, Lord Jesus!"

In September of 1977, a crowd of 50,000 Christians assembled in Kansas City. The speaker, sensing the mood of his audience, lifted his Bible high into the air as he said, "If you sneak a peek at the back of the Book, Jesus wins!" And the great crowd roared their approval with ten minutes of cheering and applause.

Yes, friend! Jesus will win! And you and I can be on the winning side if we choose. Sin and rebellion and heartache and death are on the way out—all because of Jesus. Life, never-ending life, can be yours if you want it. You can choose it now—by choosing Him!

Identification, Please

Ernest Digweed was a retired teacher. He lived alone in a small house in Portsmouth, England, and had no known relatives. A neighbor said he "didn't dress or look like a wealthy man, kept very much to himself and hardly ever spoke to anyone." He was eighty-one when he died in 1976.

But it turns out that he left a rather strange will. He left $44,000 for Jesus Christ on the occasion of His return to this earth.

And Mr. Digweed wanted to be sure the money didn't go astray. So he specified that Christ, in order to claim it, must return within the next eighty years. He must return specifically "to reign on earth." And he must prove His identity to the British government. There are those who think that may not be so easy.

His probate attorney said, "I certainly anticipate we are going to have a lot of trouble, particularly with cranks." And he asked anyone who might be listening, "Who can tell who is the real Jesus Christ? Different people think different things."

Personally I don't think Jesus Christ will ever collect the money—or make an attempt to collect it. He won't need it then, though he could use it now.

But on this matter of identity, I have the distinct impression that when Christ returns it will be we, not He, who will have to produce identification. And for some of us it will be difficult—in fact, impossible. Some of us just won't get in!

Jesus said as much. He was talking about the day of judg-

145

ment one day, and He said, "Not everyone who says to me, 'Lord, Lord,' will enter the kingdom of heaven, but only he who does the will of my Father who is in heaven. Many will say to me on that day, 'Lord, Lord, did we not prophesy in your name, and in your name drive out demons and perform many miracles?' Then I will tell them plainly, 'I never knew you. Away from me, you evildoers!' " Matthew 7:21-23, NIV.

Picture them fumbling in their wallets for some identification. But a driver's license won't help then. A bank card won't help then. Nothing in a man's wallet will help him then!

"But, Lord, You remember us. We're the ones who worked so hard for You. We prophesied in Your name. We cast out demons. We worked a lot of miracles. Don't You recognize us, Lord?"

But He says, "No, I never knew you. You are none of Mine. If you were Mine, you would have done My Father's will."

And the door is shut. They are turned away. The One they have professed to serve doesn't even recognize them!

Evidently, Heaven values obedience more than activity. More than prophesying. More than casting out demons. More than miracles!

Mr. Digweed was being a little presumptuous, don't you think, to set up the conditions that Christ must meet? It's Christ who sets up the conditions—for *us* to meet.

There's this eighty-year business—that Christ must return in the next eighty years if He was to claim Mr. Digweed's money. That troubles me too. Because Mr. Digweed has it backward. It's God who sets the time of His return. That's God's business. Our business is to be ready for the deadline, even though we don't know when it may be. Mr. Digweed has God's business and our business mixed up.

Let me remind you that Jesus said, "Of that day and hour no one knows, not even the angels of heaven, nor the Son, but the Father alone." Matthew 24:36, NASB.

No one knows when Christ will return. But people keep setting dates. Some talk about the year 2000. And some say 1999. And Mr. Digweed suggests an eighty-year limit. And it troubles me.

Why? It troubles me, first of all, because, according to the word of Jesus, date-setting is an exercise in futility. What troubles me more is that these are all such comfortable dates. They give us a lot of time to get ready. And what if we don't have a lot of time?

God has an enemy. We have an enemy. We call him Satan. He's a clever deceiver. And he'd like to see us all lose out. He'd like nothing better than for us to think we have a lot of time when we don't. He'd like to see us surprised, fatally surprised, by the return of Christ. He'd like to see us unprepared. He'd like to see us miss all the good things God has in mind for us in the future life.

Tell me, how would you live if you thought Christ wouldn't return for a hundred years? Or eighty? Or fifty?

But how would you live if you thought He *might* return this year? You get the point.

Back to the matter of identification. I say again, when Christ returns, He won't need to prove His identity. Everybody on this earth will know who He is. Everybody on this earth will be watching as He appears in the skies. And not a soul will have to ask who He is!

The apostle John, in the book of Revelation, says of that day, "Look, he is coming with the clouds, and every eye will see him . . . ; and all the peoples of the earth will mourn because of him." Revelation 1:7, NIV.

There will be no problem, *then,* in knowing who He is!

But in the meantime, between now and then, there is a very real problem. Because Jesus said that in these last days we would be bombarded with people claiming to be Christ. And what if we don't know how to tell the real Christ from a pretender? What if we don't know how to spot a counterfeit? What if we attach ourselves to an impostor, thinking him to be Christ?

Jesus warned us that it could happen. He said, "At that time if anyone says to you, 'Look, here is the Christ!' or, 'There he is!' do not believe it. For false Christs and false prophets will appear and perform great signs and miracles to deceive even the elect—if that were possible. See, I have told you ahead of time. So if anyone tells you, 'There he is, out in the desert,' do not go out; or, 'Here he is, in the inner rooms,' do not believe it." Matthew 24:23-26, NIV.

Evidently this is serious. Because, according to Jesus, the deceptions of these last days will not be crude and clumsy. He wasn't talking about a few cranks that anybody could see through. Evidently these impostors will bring in miracles, the supernatural, to back up their claims. And evidently these pretenders will be so clever that almost everybody will be fooled!

It will be, in a way, like the TV game of yesteryear, "To Tell the Truth." One impostor after another will tell his story and make his claims. And they will have prepared well. And the panel—nearly everybody on earth—will be fooled!

And when the real Christ stands up, it will be a sad, embarrassing, eternally tragic day. Because almost everybody on earth will already have attached himself to the most effective of the pretenders—and bowed down to him, thinking him to be Christ!

How can we be sure? How can we keep from making such a tragic mistake? The danger is not that we mistake the real Christ for a counterfeit. No one will do that. The danger is that, before the real Christ appears in the skies, we shall already have been fooled, already shall have taken our place under the banner of a pretender to the throne of the Lord Jesus Christ!

You say, "I'm not easily fooled." You say, "I seem to have a sixth sense—or maybe it's intuition. I can spot a fake anywhere."

Then you're just the person I'm worried about. Because the time is coming when we can't go by our senses. We won't be able to decide the great issues ahead by a sixth sense. Or by intuition. Or by a hunch!

You say, "I could tell by his appearance."

But the apostle Paul said that "Satan himself masquerades as an angel of light." 2 Corinthians 11:14, NIV.

And if Satan can masquerade as an angel of light, he can also masquerade as Christ. And he will! So you can't go by appearance.

You say, "I could tell by his voice." But could you? Paul said, "There are . . . so many kinds of voices in the world." 1 Corinthians 14:10, KJV.

So many kinds of voices. And so many imitators. Is Satan less skillful than those we have heard? So you can't go by the voice.

You say, "I could just feel whether it's right or wrong."

But a very wise man said, "There is a way which seems right to a man, but its end is the way of death." Proverbs 14:12, NASB.

So you can't go by how it seems.

You say, "If he worked a miracle, I'd know he was the real Christ."

But wait, Jesus said that the false christs would "perform great signs and miracles." Remember?

And the apostle John, in the book of Revelation, speaks of "spirits of devils, working miracles." Revelation 16:14, KJV.

In the days of Elijah fire came down from heaven to show who was the true God. But in the last days fire will come down from heaven to back up the claims of a false god. An agent of Satan, says John, will perform "great and miraculous signs, even causing fire to come down from heaven to earth in full view of men." Revelation 13:13, NIV.

So you can't go by miracles. To go by miracles could be most dangerous of all!

You say, "If he quotes Scripture, I'll know he's the real Christ."

But Satan quoted Scripture to Jesus in that confrontation in the wilderness above Jordan. Remember? So you can't go by that.

Then how can you tell? There's only one way. It's by the way the Word of God is handled, the way the Scripture is used. Said the prophet Isaiah, "To the law and to the testimony: if they speak not according to this word, it is because there is no light in them." Isaiah 8:20, KJV.

The real Christ will not misquote Scripture. He will not misapply it. He will not twist it. He will not disagree with it. He will not contradict it. He will not say He came to change it. He will not suggest the slightest doubt about the authority of God's written Word!

Did you know that this is how Jesus recognized Satan in that confrontation in the wilderness? The visitor looked like an angel, talked like an angel, seemed to be an angel. But Jesus recognized him as His archenemy by the way he misquoted Scripture, by the way he twisted it and misapplied it. He recognized him by the subtle insinuations of doubt. He recognized him immediately when he said, "*If* You are the Son of God."

Yes, the real Christ will speak in perfect harmony with the written Word of God. And you can go by that!

But that isn't all. Not only will the real Christ *speak* in harmony with Scripture. He will *return* in harmony with Scripture. He will return in the *way* the Bible says He will return.

You see, the Bible tells us in detail *how* Christ will return.

According to the Bible, Jesus left this earth in a cloud. And He will return in the same way. "After he said this, he was taken up before their very eyes, and a cloud hid him from their sight. They were looking intently up into the sky as he was going, when suddenly two men dressed in white stood beside them. 'Men of Galilee,' they said, 'why do you stand here looking into the sky? This same Jesus, who has been taken from you into heaven, will come back in the same way you have seen him go into heaven.'" Acts 1:9-11, NIV.

Jesus said His coming would be like the lightning, easily seen. "As the lightning comes from the east and flashes to the west, so will be the coming of the Son of Man." Matthew 24:27, NIV.

Jesus said that when He comes He will bring "all the angels with him." Matthew 25:31, NIV.

And remember that John said of His coming, "Every eye will see him." Revelation 1:7, NIV.

According to the apostle Paul—and it's important to remember—that the feet of Jesus do not even touch the ground. His people are caught up into the cloud to meet Him. We read, "The Lord himself will come down from heaven, with a loud command, with the voice of the archangel and with the trumpet call of God, and the dead in Christ will rise first. After that, we who are still alive and are left will be caught up with them in the clouds to meet the Lord in the air. And so we will be with the Lord forever." 1 Thessalonians 4:16, 17, NIV.

Our God has given us this information so that we need not be deceived. Satan will impersonate Christ. He will try to counter-

feit His coming. But God will not permit him to counterfeit the
way that Christ returns.

I think now you see the problem. If we don't know our Bibles,
how will we know when Scripture is misquoted or misused? If
we don't know our Bibles, how will we know *how* the real
Christ will return? If we don't know our Bibles, how can we spot
an impostor? If we don't know our Bibles, what will keep us
from deception? What will keep us from bowing down to an impostor, perhaps even Satan himself, thinking him to be Christ?

Do you see why it's dangerous business to neglect the study of
our Bibles? Do you see how risky it is to leave the study of God's
Word to others—and not know it for ourselves?

One of these days you personally may be in the audience of a
brilliant being who claims to be Christ. If you let your eyes decide it, he is the real Christ. If you let your ears decide it, he is
the real Christ. If you let your feelings decide it, he is the real
Christ. But if you let the Word of God decide it, he is one of the
masquerading pretenders that Jesus talked about!

The tragedy is that millions won't apply that test. Millions
will be fascinated by the charisma of the impostor. Millions will
be trapped by the subtle suggestion that maybe the Scriptures
are not a safe guide. Millions will go by their senses. And millions will be fooled. Eventually almost everybody—before the
real Christ ever appears—will have knelt in worship at the feet
of the master impostor. They will think they are worshiping
their Saviour!

But let me say once more, When the real Christ appears,
after the pretenders have had their day, there will be no question about His identity. Everybody will know!

To show you what I mean, let me share with you just a few
paragraphs from a description of that day that must have been
inspired. It reads like an eyewitness account. Listen!

"It is at midnight that God manifests His power for the deliverance of His people. The sun appears, shining in its strength.

Signs and wonders follow in quick succession. The wicked
look with terror and amazement upon the scene, while the righ-
teous behold with solemn joy the tokens of their deliverance.
Everything in nature seems turned out of its course. The

streams cease to flow. Dark, heavy clouds come up, and clash against each other. In the midst of the angry heavens is one clear space of indescribable glory, whence comes the voice of God like the sound of many waters, saying: 'It is done.' Revelation 16:17.

"That voice shakes the heavens and the earth. There is a mighty earthquake. . . . The firmament appears to open and shut. The glory from the throne of God seems flashing through. The mountains shake like a reed in the wind, and ragged rocks are scattered on every side. There is a roar as of a coming tempest. The sea is lashed into fury. There is heard the shriek of the hurricane, like the voice of demons upon a mission of destruction. The whole earth heaves and swells like the waves of the sea. Its surface is breaking up. Its very foundations seem to be giving way. Mountain chains are sinking. Inhabited islands disappear. . . . The proudest cities of the earth are laid low. . . .

"Soon there appears in the east a small black cloud, about half the size of a man's hand. It is the cloud which surrounds the Saviour and which seems in the distance to be shrouded in darkness. The people of God know this to be the sign of the Son of man. In solemn silence they gaze upon it as it draws nearer the earth, becoming lighter and more glorious, until it is a great white cloud, its base a glory like consuming fire. . . . Jesus rides forth as a mighty conqueror. . . . With anthems of celestial melody the holy angels, a vast, unnumbered throng, attend Him on His way. The firmament seems filled with radiant forms. . . . No human pen can portray the scene; no mortal mind is adequate to conceive its splendor."

I have been quoting from *The Great Controversy*, by Ellen White. And I believe it's going to happen just that way. If you would like to read more of this amazing, gripping, thrilling description, you may order it from the publishers of the book you now hold in your hands.

And now let me remind you that there's no better time than now—this moment—to start getting acquainted with the lovely Jesus, the one who loves you so much that He died for you. Become so well acquainted with Him that you can never be fooled by any pretender! Tomorrow may be too late.

The Writing on the Wall

The handwriting on the wall. What do we mean by those words? Do we mean that something or somebody is finished—or about to be? Do we mean that something terrible is about to happen, unless evasive action is taken? Or do we mean that something frightfully decisive has already happened, and nothing can change it? Is it a warning—or an irrevocable verdict?

There is tension in the courtroom. The jury is filing in. Breathlessly everyone waits for the fateful word. And then it comes. Guilty. Or not guilty. The reporters rush to the phones. The defendant, overjoyed, collapses into the arms of loved ones and walks out a free man. Or, when all the excitement has died away, when the reporters and their microphones have gone, he is left in a silent, lonely cell to contemplate what the decision of the jurors has done to his life.

He has had no vote in that decision. He wasn't present when it was made. He wasn't even aware of the moment when his fate was decided. Yet he had determined it by his own previous performance.

It is that way with many of life's big moments. Decisions are made that may affect our lives for years to come. But we hear no siren, no tolling bell, no signal that a decision is being made. We aren't there. We have no vote. Only by our past performance can we influence the outcome.

It was that way with the handwriting on the wall. It really happened, you know. It happened to an ancient king by the name of Belshazzar.

Belshazzar was a proud and arrogant king. True, the armies of the Medes and Persians were camped outside the city. But Babylon's wall could withstand any attack that might be made. And the city had food in abundance. And so the king, with a reckless feeling of security, made a great feast one night.

All the trappings of wealth and power gave splendor to the scene. Beautiful women were there. Men of genius were there. Princes and statesmen were there. And they drank wine like water.

The king himself took the lead in the riotous orgy. He seemed to be seeking for some act of ultimate recklessness. And finally, maddened by wine, he thought of it. He remembered the utensils of gold and silver that his grandfather had brought from the temple in Jerusalem. He and his guests would drink from these. Nothing was too sacred for him to handle—no act of blasphemy beyond him.

But an unseen watcher noted it all. And suddenly, when the revelry was at its height, a bloodless hand began to write upon the wall in letters of fire. Every sound was hushed. The king and his guests watched in nameless terror as the mysterious characters were formed. Not an eye could turn away. No witty remarks now. No reckless blasphemy now. Only pale faces and cries of fear.

You remember the story. Not a soul present at that feast could read the flaming message. And then the queen mother remembered Daniel, the Hebrew captive. Daniel was brought in. And Daniel could read it. He said to the proud king, "This is the interpretation of the thing: MENE; God hath numbered thy kingdom, and finished it. TEKEL; Thou art weighed in the balances, and art found wanting. PERES; Thy kingdom is divided, and given to the Medes and Persians." Daniel 5:26-28, KJV.

Weighed in the balances . . . and found wanting. God didn't say, "Belshazzar, you'd better be careful and change your ways or you're going to be in trouble." No, the weighing had already been done. The decision had already been made—in a moment of which Belshazzar was completely unaware. A moment that would have struck terror to his heart had he known.

Also unknown to the king, the armies of Cyrus had diverted

the waters of the Euphrates River. The river ran right through the city, you recall. Then they entered the city by way of the riverbed and through gates that had been left unlocked—just as God had predicted they would be. Then they stormed the palace. And Belshazzar lost his life—with no opportunity then to repent!

What does all this have to do with us? Very much. So much that Jesus spent considerable time trying to warn us of our danger.

Come with me to the twenty-fourth and twenty-fifth chapters of Matthew. We usually think of these two chapters as a discussion only of the return of Christ to this earth. But there is more.

And right in the middle of this discussion Jesus made a statement that we often hear quoted. He said, "Then shall two be in the field; the one shall be taken, and the other left. Two women shall be grinding at the mill; the one shall be taken, and the other left." Matthew 24:40, 41, KJV.

Millions of sincere Christians believe that Jesus was talking about what they call the rapture—the secret rapture. They believe that those who are ready to meet their Lord are going to be caught away—silently and secretly—and all the rest left here.

We see bumper stickers that say, "If I'm raptured, take the wheel." Imagination has constructed vivid descriptions of automobiles that go careening down freeways without drivers. Of trains that plunge through red lights and off open drawbridges, with their loads of panic-stricken passengers—because the engineer has been raptured. Of airline pilots suddenly disappearing through the walls of the cockpit, leaving the passengers hysterical as they plunge earthward.

It would seem that if something of this kind is likely to occur, then for the safety of the general public we ought to have legislation that all pilots and engineers and school-bus drivers be non-Christians. Wouldn't you think?

Now, I'm not ridiculing this belief. These people are just as sincere as I am. And I can see how they have come to interpret the statement of our Lord as they have. I only ask, Could they be mistaken—at least in part? And could it be a dangerous mistake? Could Jesus be trying to tell us something that we desperately need to understand?

Whatever Jesus is trying to tell us in these chapters, He tries repeatedly. He uses one illustration after another to get His point across. He seems to be concerned, above all else, that we watch, that we be alert, that we not be surprised, that we not be caught unaware.

Surprised by what? By His coming? Yes, millions will be. Most of the world will be surprised, though not a single man or woman needs to be. The warning will have been sufficient. The warning will have been urgent. The announcement of His coming, of its approach, will have been flashed around the world by thousands of voices.

Surprised? Yes. But will anyone be *unaware* of His coming when it happens—*unaware* that it is happening? Could it possibly be a secret event, a secret happening—unknown except to those involved? Hardly!

Remember the words of the apostle Paul: "For the Lord himself shall descend from heaven with a shout, with the voice of the archangel, and with the trump of God." 1 Thessalonians 4:16, KJV.

The apostle John says, "Every eye shall see him . . . and all kindreds of the earth shall wail because of him." Revelation 1:7, KJV.

Every living soul on earth will be watching. And those not ready to meet their Lord will wail at the sight of His face. Not a soul, anywhere on earth, will be unaware of what is happening. Does that sound like a secret rapture? No. Just the opposite!

And listen to this description of that fateful hour: "And there were voices, and thunders, and lightnings; and there was a great earthquake, such as was not since men were upon the earth, so mighty an earthquake, and so great. . . . And the cities of the nations fell. . . . And every island fled away, and the mountains were not found. And there fell upon men a great hail out of heaven, every stone about the weight of a talent: and men blasphemed God because of the plague of the hail; for the plague thereof was exceeding great." Revelation 16:18-21, KJV.

Could anyone be unaware of all that? Could all that be kept secret? No. That would be impossible. The return of Christ to this earth will be the most vocal, the most spectacular event of all time. And not a soul will miss it!

But is it possible that something does happen *before* the return of Christ—something frightfully important—of which almost the whole world is unaware? Is that what we need to understand?

It is true that, when Christ returns, those who are ready to meet Him will be *taken*—to be with their Lord, taken to the home He has prepared for them. And everyone else, all the unprepared, will be *left*—strewn over the face of this desolate earth, as we shall see in our next chapter.

But listen, when will it be *decided* who is to be taken and who is to be left? On the spot? No. That decision must necessarily have been made before hand. Says Jesus, "Behold, I am coming soon! My reward is with me, and I will give to everyone according to what he has done." Revelation 22:12, NIV.

How can Jesus bring His rewards with Him unless some decision has already been made as to who shall have those rewards and who shall not? Must there not have been an accounting? Says the apostle John, "And I saw the dead, small and great, stand before God; and the books were opened; and another book was opened, which is the book of life: and the dead were judged out of those things which were written in the books, according to their works." Revelation 20:12, KJV.

How can dead men stand before God? By the record of their lives. By what is written in the books.

Evidently every one of us, before Jesus returns, will be judged out of the books, without our being physically present, and at a time of which we are completely unaware. We won't know that it is happening.

And as those decisions are made, some of us will be marked to be *taken*, and some to be *left*. But we won't go anywhere—not right then. Two men in the field will go right on working together as before, and two women at the mill will go on grinding as before—unaware that anything has happened.

Let's get the background of this discussion in these two chapters of the book of Matthew. I believe we can better understand what Jesus is trying to get across.

The twenty-fourth chapter begins with Jesus and His disciples leaving the temple. The disciples remark about the magnificence of the building, and Jesus tells them it will one day be destroyed—not one stone left on another. They think nothing but the end of the world could accomplish such destruction, so they ask Him how they can tell when the end of the world is near.

Now, actually Jesus is talking about the destruction of Jerusalem which would take place in A.D. 70, so He continues to talk about the destruction of Jerusalem. But He also answers their question about signs of the end of the world, how they can know when His coming is near. The two subjects are intertwined in this chapter, with some of his statements having a double application—that is, applying both to the destruction of Jerusalem and the end of the world. Jesus also talks in this chapter about a long period of persecution that would come to His people. So you see more than one subject is covered here.

But it's the illustrations that Jesus used that will give us the key to a better understanding. So let's look at the illustrations.

Just before the statement about one being taken and the other left, Jesus is talking about Noah's Flood. He uses that as an illustration. He says the people of that day went right on with eating and drinking and marrying, with the routine of everyday life, "and knew not until the flood came, and took them all away." Matthew 24:39, KJV.

What didn't they know? That the Flood was coming? True, it took them by surprise, even though they'd been told for 120 years that it would happen.

But there was something else they didn't know. They didn't know that seven days before it started to rain, their destiny had been sealed. Seven days before, Noah had pleaded with them for the last time to enter the ship he had built and avoid destruction. But they had refused. Then Noah and his family had gone in. And then the people had witnessed a very strange sight.

There was a flash of dazzling light. A cloud brighter than the lightning descended from heaven and hovered before the entrance. The massive door was swung in place by unseen hands. Noah was shut in. The mocking world was shut out. God had shut the door. And God alone could open it!

But that was not the end of the world for those people. They soon recovered from their fright and returned to their ridicule of Noah. For seven days the sun shone as usual and everything seemed normal. Then came the Flood. But the door had been shut, their destiny sealed—seven days before!

Then Jesus talks about a thief entering the house at night. We don't expect a thief. We may not be aware when the thief breaks in. We may not know till morning that we have been robbed of our valued possessions.

Do you begin to see what Jesus is trying to tell us?

In the twenty-fifth chapter, He talks about ten virgins, and five of them weren't ready. They went to get oil for their lamps and then tried to go in to the wedding. But the door had been shut. A shut door again. Do you see?

Then Jesus, still in this twenty-fifth chapter, talks about a householder leaving money with each of his servants and going on a trip. When he comes back, he calls them to account for the way they have handled the money. An accounting. A reckoning. A judgment, you might say.

Later on in this chapter Jesus says that when He comes in the clouds of heaven there will be a separation. The angels, He says, will separate those who are ready to meet Him from those who are not—just as a shepherd divides the sheep from the goats.

In all these illustrations there is the element of a separation. Those who went into Noah's boat, and those who did not. Those who were surprised by the thief and those who were not. The virgins who were ready and those who were not. The servants who handled their master's money wisely and those who did not. But remember, in Noah's day, how the door was shut? And that wasn't the end of the world for them. But that's when their destiny was sealed. When the door was shut. And they were unaware.

Tell me. When Jesus comes down through the flaming skies,

the angels will make a separation. But how can they do that if the destiny of each individual has not already been decided, settled, sealed, at some previous time? If there is to be a separation when Jesus comes, there must first have been an accounting, a decision, a verdict.

Do you see what Jesus is trying to tell us? He's trying to tell us that not only is it important to be ready when He comes and not be surprised. He's also trying to tell us that *before* He comes, at a time of which we are unaware, there will be an accounting of every man's record. There will be a reckoning. There will be a judgment. And we won't be there. We won't even know when it happens. That's why He keeps telling us to be alert, to watch, to be ready. That's what He's warning us about. And what could possibly be more important, more vital, more eternally decisive?

"One shall be taken, and the other left," said Jesus. As the result of the judgment, one is marked to be taken, and the other marked to be left. One is convicted and one is acquitted. One is found guilty, and the other, because of the saving blood of Jesus, is found not guilty.

But neither one goes anywhere right then. The two men in the field go right on working. The two women at the mill go right on grinding. Not a one of them knows that anything has happened. They are completely unaware that their names have come up in judgment and their cases decided.

Do you get the picture? There is no peal of thunder to mark the hour when our cases—yours and mine—are decided. No tolling bells. No siren. No signal. Nothing. Silently, unnoticed as the midnight thief, the fateful moment arrives—and then is gone. No one sees the writing on the wall. But it is there. No one hears the words of a disappointed Saviour. But to many a man He is forced to say, "You've been weighed in the balances, and found wanting!"

What a message! What a warning! No wonder Jesus tried so hard to get it across!

Has the thought crossed your mind that there is something unfair about judging us when we aren't there to answer for ourselves? No, friend. It isn't unfair. There's Someone there to represent you. Someone to represent me. So it's all right!

Suppose I ask, Who will represent me? The apostle John? But John wanted to call down fire on people who did wrong. The apostle Peter? But Peter cut off a man's ear with his sword in an implusive moment. Not Peter. The apostle Paul? But Paul was so educated. Maybe he wouldn't understand me. Jesus? And my heart thrills with relief. Jesus! He's my best Friend! I know Him! I talk to Him every day! He loved me so much that He died for me—even when I didn't love Him! If it's Jesus, it's all right!

But suppose I don't know Him! I say, "Jesus? Oh, no. I don't know Him. He's a stranger to me. He wanted to be friends. He wanted to save me. And I wouldn't let Him! No! Not Jesus!" And I know in my heart of hearts that I'm guilty. I'm lost. Not because I was a thief or a murderer. Not because I didn't live a respectable life. But because I turned my back on Him. I rejected Him. He wanted to save me. And I wouldn't let Him!

Friend, He wants to save *you*. He wants to represent *you*. Will you let Him?

The Rattle
of the Keys

In the year 1860 Marcellin Berthelot, the French chemist, predicted that within a hundred years scientists would understand the atom. And he believed that when science should reach that stage, God would soon come down to earth with His big ring of keys and say to humanity, "Gentlemen, it is closing time!"

Today we can hear the rattle of the keys. Do you have any plans for after hours?

A televised discussion of the energy crisis aired recently was introduced by an imaginary scene depicting the day energy runs out. Two sinister-looking men approached a normally lighted American home and rang the doorbell. They were greeted by a young man with his wife and children. The young father asked simply, "Now?" And they answered, "Now."

The men proceeded through the house disconnecting and making inoperable every appliance. Small appliances were placed in bags and carried away. Larger ones were chained and padlocked. When they had finished, they turned off the power and left the little family in complete darkness. The father said, "I thought we'd have more time."

And one of the children asked, "Daddy, will we freeze in the dark?"

It may not happen as dramatically as that. But it may happen sooner than we think!

I would like you to consider a day far more serious, far more devastating.

163

We've had our emergencies—blackouts, transportation strikes, teacher strikes, doctor strikes, teamster strikes. Houses have been burned, flooded, shaken down by earthquakes. Fog has closed our airports. Ice has crippled our cities.

But put these all together, if you will. Combine them into one grand emergency—worldwide. Try to imagine what it will be like the day *everything* stops. We may or may not run out of energy. We may or may not experience famine. We *will* run out of time. The last grain of sand will run through the hourglass. And no power on earth will be able to turn it over and start it again!

Millions, in those last irreversible hours, will say to God, "Now, Lord?" and He'll say, "Yes, now." And those same millions, pitiful in their disappointment, will say to each other, "I thought we'd have more time!"

Do you realize that one day soon, within the space of a few short hours, this earth will be depopulated—empty—with not one human being left alive anywhere on the planet? The prophet Isaiah describes that day: "Behold, the Lord maketh the earth empty, and maketh it waste . . . , and scattereth abroad the inhabitants thereof." Isaiah 24:1-3, KJV.

Evidently when God decides it is closing time, He will lock up this planet and leave it empty, uninhabited—without even a "For Rent" sign!

This is how the prophet Jeremiah describes the scene: "The slain of the Lord shall be at that day from one end of the earth even unto the other end of the earth: they shall not be lamented, neither gathered, nor buried." Jeremiah 25:33, KJV.

What a picture! Dead bodies strewn all over this planet, unburied. Why aren't they buried? Evidently because there is no one to bury them.

What does all this mean? Does it mean that the annihilation the doomsday peddlers have talked about has really happened? Does it mean that God, in His anger, has come down and wiped out the human race as in the days of Noah—but this time without leaving even eight people to start over? No, it doesn't, as we shall see.

The prophet Jeremiah tells us more. He says, "I beheld the

earth, and, lo, it was without form, and void; and the heavens, and they had no light. I beheld the mountains, and, lo, they trembled, and all the hills moved lightly. I beheld, and, lo, there was no man, and all the birds of the heavens were fled." Jeremiah 4:23-25, KJV.

The earth here is said to be "without form, and void." That's the way it is described in the first chapter of Genesis, before the creation of this planet was complete. The earth is also described, on this day in the future, as being dark. It says the heavens have no light. It says there is no man, and even the birds have fled.

It also says here that the mountains are trembling—evidently from some great event. What has happened? We read on: "I beheld, and, lo, the fruitful place was a wilderness, and all the cities thereof were broken down *at the presence of the Lord,* and by his fierce anger. For thus hath the Lord said, The whole land shall be desolate; yet will I not make a full end." Jeremiah 4:26, 27, KJV.

Notice that here is a ray of hope. God says, "Yet will I not make a full end." Evidently God still has plans for this planet!

But what has happened that leaves the earth in such an empty, desolate condition? It says cities have been broken down at the presence of the Lord. Evidently our Lord has returned to this earth. For we read in the book of Revelation that at the time of Christ's return, "there was a great earthquake, such as was not since men were upon the earth, so mighty an earthquake, and so great. . . . And the cities of the nations fell." Revelation 16:18, 19, KJV.

That's how the cities fell. And that's why the mountains are still shaking. The planet is suffering the aftershocks of the greatest earthquake it has ever experienced.

But now the hope comes into this picture. Because if Christ has returned, is it possible that not *all* the inhabitants of the earth have been strewn dead over its surface, but that some of them, a good many of them, have gone somewhere?

You may be saying, "Pastor Vandeman, I thought that when Christ returns He would set up His kingdom on the earth and we would have a thousand years of peace. I'm confused."

Yes, you recall that when Christ was here as a man, even His own disciples were confused about His mission. They thought He had come to set up an earthly kingdom at that time. But He hadn't. He had come to die on the cross in man's place, to make salvation possible.

Just so, there is confusion in many minds about what happens when Christ returns in the near future. There will be a millennium, all right. Incidentally, the word "millennium" simply means a thousand years. But during that thousand years there will be no kingdom of Christ set up on this earth. And it will mean no second chance for sinners. When Christ returns—even before He returns—every sinner will have had his last chance. And that's it. Sinners can't very easily repent while they are strewn over the earth dead!

Christ will set up His kingdom on earth. But not yet!

Do you remember what Jesus said about the purpose of His return? Let's read those familiar words again: "Set your troubled hearts at rest. . . . There are many dwelling-places in my Father's house; if it were not so I should have told you, for I am going there on purpose to prepare a place for you. And if I go and prepare a place for you, I shall come again and receive you to myself, so that where I am you may be also." John 14:1-3, NEB.

Where did Jesus say He was going when He left this earth? To His Father's house. Where is that? He often spoke of His Father as being in heaven. Why was Jesus going there? On purpose to prepare a place for His people. And why would He return to this earth? To get His people and take them to the place He has prepared—to heaven. That's perfectly clear, isn't it?

Notice that He said nothing about setting up a kingdom at that time—or even spending any time here. He would just come to get His people.

Let's read again the apostle Paul's description of the day that Christ returns, and see if it agrees. Of course you know it will. He says, "The Lord Himself will descend from heaven with a shout, with the voice of the archangel, and with the trumpet of God; and the dead in Christ shall rise first. Then we who are alive and remain shall be caught up together with them in the clouds to meet the Lord in the air, and thus we shall always be with the Lord." 1 Thessalonians 4:16, 17, NASB.

Do you see? He comes back to get His people, just as He said He would. Many of them, millions of them, have died through the ages. So He calls them to life. And they, together with those of His people who are still living, are caught up into the cloud to meet Him. Christ and His people are united, never to part again.

See how clear it is? It's like a young man who comes by to take his girl friend out for the evening. He stops in front of the house. She's watching for him. She runs out to the car. He helps her in. He doesn't even come into the house.

So with Jesus. All His people—those still living and those who have died—are lifted into the cloud to meet Him. And His feet don't even touch the ground!

Don't forget that point. It's important. Jesus said there would be false christs, counterfeit christs, in these last days. Remember? But when you hear of someone here on this earth claiming to be Christ, you know without even investigating that he's a counterfeit. Because the feet of the real Christ, when He comes, will not even touch the ground!

So now you see that the entire human race isn't strewn over the earth. Rather, millions have gone somewhere with their Lord. They'll be gone for a thousand years. And then they'll be back. Because God has plans for this earth and for His people. And He has an account that must finally be settled with rebellion.

Why are the rest left behind, strewn over the earth? Is it because God wanted to leave them behind? No. Jesus died for every one of them. He made provision for every one of them. There is room in His Father's house for every one of them. His heart will grieve over every one of them. He doesn't want a one to be lost. But these have refused to accept His sacrifice in their place. These have refused to let Him save them. And He will not force the will.

These have had no plans for after closing time. And so, in the final hours, they have had no shelter. They have been unable to survive the glory and the guilt of that day. The glory of His coming, and the guilt in their hearts—a guilt that He wanted to forgive—have been too much for them!

Too often, I'm afraid, we make synonyms out of the return of Christ and the end of the world. We speak of the return of Christ and the end of the world and the end of time and doomsday—and use all those phrases interchangeably. We make the return of Christ sound so inevitably final. And it is—for those who have no plans for after hours, for after the planet is locked up and left empty and deserted.

But it doesn't need to be final at all. For those who love their Lord, who have accepted His sacrifice, closing time doesn't mean the end. It doesn't lock them out of anything. It opens the doors and sets them free as they've never been free before. Their responsibilities and cares and toil are over. They've put in their hours of watching. Now comes what they've been living for, waiting for!

Closing time, then, means different things to different people. You who work in an office know what that means. Some have plans and interests and dreams for after hours. Some don't. There are those who have no interests outside of working hours. Their friends, their social life, their consuming interests are all locked within the office walls. When they leave, they enter a silent, lonely world. But others look forward to the evening with great anticipation. Tonight they will be with someone they love. Closing time will not end their day!

But let's follow through now with just what happens. Does the Bible really say that God's people will be with Him in heaven for a thousand years? Yes. It does. It says concerning His people, "They lived and reigned with Christ a thousand years." Revelation 20:4, KJV.

But what happens to all those people strewn over the earth? Do we ever hear from them again? Yes. The very next verse tells us what happens to them. It says, The rest of the dead lived not again until the thousand years were finished.

This may sound a little confusing. But it will straighten out for us in just a moment. The rest of the dead, it says, lived not again until the thousand years were finished. Who are the rest of the dead?

The apostle Paul has told us, you remember, that when Christ returns His people who have died will be resurrected and lifted into the cloud to be with Him. Now it is telling us here in Revelation that the rest of the dead—the dead who have not accepted Christ, the dead who were not resurrected at Christ's coming, and the dead who are strewn over the surface of the earth because they couldn't stand the glory of His coming—these, it says, will not live again *until* the thousand years are finished.

Notice that word "until." They will not live again *until* the thousand years are finished. Then evidently they will live *after* the thousand years are finished. Evidently there are two resurrections. Referring to the resurrection of God's people, which we have already seen takes place at Christ's coming, it says here in the fifth verse, "This is the first resurrection." So the second resurrection, at the end of the thousand years, must involve those who have rejected Christ.

Incidentally, this twentieth chapter of Revelation, from which we are reading, is the only place in the Bible where the thousand-year period is mentioned.

So now you get the picture. All God's people are with Him in heaven. All those who have chosen to be lost are dead. And the earth is empty, desolate, for a thousand years.

Empty, that is, so far as human beings are concerned. But there are some nonhumans here—one in particular. Listen to this: "I saw an angel come down from heaven, having the key of the bottomless pit and a great chain in his hand. And he laid hold on the dragon, that old serpent, which is the Devil, and Satan, and bound him a thousand years, and cast him into the bottomless pit, and shut him up, and set a seal upon him, that he should deceive the nations no more, till the thousand years should be fulfilled; and after that he must be loosed a little season." Revelation 20:1-3, KJV.

What does this mean? You couldn't lock Satan up, of course, with a literal key or restrain him with a literal chain. And no bottomless pit, no yawning chasm, could hold him. This is a symbolic way of saying that the activities of Satan will at last be brought to a halt. They will be halted by the fact that he and his angels are confined to this earth, not permitted to go anywhere else. And since every human being is either gone or dead, he is chained, completely restrained, by the fact that there is absolutely no one here to tempt. He and his rebel angels will have a thousand years to wander over the dark, desolate, empty, ruined earth and see the havoc they have caused! Satan at last is a victim of his folly.

In the meantime, God's people will be spending a thousand happy years in heaven, in the fantastically beautiful place the Saviour has prepared for them. And during those years there will be plenty of time to understand God's dealing with those who are lost, with loved ones who are not there—to understand that not one person has been lost that God could possibly save without forcing the will. For every single one He has done all it was possible to do!

And then the time comes when the account with rebellion must finally be settled. God and His people descend to this earth. We read, "I John saw the holy city, new Jerusalem, coming down from God out of heaven." Revelation 21:2, KJV.

Then what happens? "When the thousand years are expired, Satan shall be loosed out of his prison, and shall go out to deceive the nations." Revelation 20:7, 8, KJV.

Satan is loosed by the fact that the second resurrection, the resurrection of the lost, has taken place. Once more the rebel host is under his control. Rebellion bursts forth in a torrent. One final attempt is made to overthrow God's government. We read: "They went up on the breadth of the earth, and compassed the camp of the saints about, and the beloved city: and fire came down from God out of heaven, and devoured them." Revelation 20:9, KJV.

That, friend, is the end of rebellion. For the good of the universe, for the good of everyone concerned, sin must be wiped out. And God uses real fire to do it. It isn't an act in which He finds pleasure. He weeps over each lost one as if he were an only child. But it has to be done.

When those flames have done their work, they will go out. Rebellion will be gone, never to trouble a happy universe again. Sin will be gone—and with it death and pain and heartache. God will give this planet, cleansed by the flames of all its pollution—God will give to His people as their permanent home. New, clean, beautiful as it was at the beginning, it will never be marred again. One pulse of harmony will beat through all God's creation. And never again will there be a discordant note!

Friend, it's almost closing time. We can hear the rattle of the keys. Do you have plans for after hours? I hope you do. The Saviour has plans for you. And listen—John, Mary, Elizabeth, Tom, whoever you are and wherever you are—think of the disappointment in the heart of the Saviour if you should be missing. No one could take the place of you. Not all the millions of the saved. Not all the adoring angels. Not all the worshiping multitudes. He wants you there. Wouldn't it be unthinkable to disappoint Him?

Winds on a Leash

For three days the long, weary hours had dragged by. Flight 316, with its sixty-eight passengers, still sat on the runway at Kennedy International Airport.

Why? Was it mechanical trouble? The weather? A hijacking? No, United States authorities only wanted to be sure that one particular passenger aboard that plane was not leaving the country against her will.

But now, in the presence of officials of both nations, she had said, "I love my husband, but he made his decision to stay here and I have made mine to leave."

Had she spoken freely, without coercion? Her husband's lawyer responded, "I couldn't say for sure. I wasn't able to tell. After all, she's an actress."

Actress or not, her decision had been made. And so after seventy-two hours, television lights went out, reporters hurried to the telephones, watching tourists turned to less exciting drama, and Flight 316 lifted into the evening sky.

That's the way God is. Holding back the flight of time. Turning aside disaster. Blunting the power of the hurricane and the flood. Restraining the winds of violence and terror and war. Holding the hourglass on a slant so that the last grains of sand will not escape. Forbidding history to sign out just yet. Unwilling to wrap it all up until every man has decided whether or not he wants to be free!

So often we have seen it happen. We have prepared for the big disaster, even for doomsday. And somehow doomsday just didn't arrive.

173

Hurricane Allen was billed as the big one—the storm of the century. A whole county was evacuated. Yet its devastation was far less than expected.

Again and again a hurricane has been aimed directly at our nation's capital. Yet nearly always the storm has veered from its expected course, leaving Washington with only its fringe of steady rain.

Why? Who restrains the fury of the storm? Who holds the winds on a leash?

Have you ever wondered what would have happened if the Arabs had won the Yom Kippur War? What if the Israelis had turned to nuclear weapons—as it is rumored they were about to do?

What if the Shah of Iran had been deposed twenty-five years earlier? Would the whole course of history have been changed?

Or what if that ill-fated attempt to rescue the American hostages in Iran had succeeded? What if there had been no dust storms that night on the Iranian desert? What if three helicopters had not failed? What if the flames of a burning jet had not lighted up the Iranian sky?

Would the hostages have been killed? Would the well-intentioned mission, if successful, have triggered World War III?

I do not know. I do know that God is still in control. History, more often than we realize, is altered by divine intervention. God has often stopped the guns of men from shooting. He has used the fog to protect men from their enemies. He works in a thousand ways that have never crossed our minds. If it were not for His restraining hand upon the winds of international terror, Armageddon would have overtaken us long before this!

It is God who says to the winds of war as He says to the waves of the sea, "hitherto shalt thou come, but no farther."

Yet one day soon the winds will be unleashed. They will blow with a fury that defies imagination. It will not be a *county* that needs to be evacuated. It will be a whole planet!

In the meantime what is happening? The book of Revelation gives us a clue:

"After this I saw four angels standing at the four corners of the earth, holding back the four winds of the earth to prevent any wind from blowing on the land or on the sea or on any tree." Revelation 7:1, NIV.

So that's it. Angels have been commissioned to hold the winds. And why?

"Then I saw another angel coming up from the east, having the seal of the living God. He called out in a loud voice to the four angels. . . 'Do not harm the land or the sea or the trees until we put a seal on the foreheads of the servants of our God.'" Verses 2, 3, NIV.

Angels are to hold back the winds, not let them blow, *until* God's people are sealed in their foreheads. With a visible mark? No. *But* many thousands of men, women and children will be so in love with Jesus that they will say, "Lord, I want to be marked as one of your children forever!"

However, other thousands—the majority, unfortunately—will say in their hearts, or by their actions, "No thank you, Lord. I know you died to save me. But I don't want to be saved. I choose to go my own way."

And when every one of us has had a chance to decide, the winds will blow. We will be ushered into a time of trouble such as this world has never known. The last grains of sand will escape the hourglass. And Jesus will return!

Decision magazine, in its June, 1980 issue, carried a beautiful and very intriguing double spread. It was a poster, really. A magnificent cloud against a deep blue sky. Above the cloud, on the left, were the words of Jesus, "Surely I am coming soon." And on the right, against the sky, were just two words: "Perhaps Today."

Perhaps today! Certainly we ought to live as if our Lord might appear at any moment. But is it really possible that He might return this very day—even before you've finished reading this book? Or are there still some Bible predictions that must be fulfilled before He appears in the skies?

I wonder if you realize how often Bible prediction has included a specific period of time. And I wonder if you realize how precisely these time prophecies have been fulfilled. Let's take a look.

Residents of this planet, in Noah's day, were to have a hundred and twenty years of probation before the Flood. That's exactly what happened. The deluge was to begin seven days after Noah entered the boat that he had built. It did. The rain would continue forty days and forty nights. It did.

God revealed to Abraham, at the time of his call, that for four hundred years his descendants would experience oppression in a strange land. They did, in Palestine and in Egypt. But 430 years after the promise to Abraham, and 400 years after the oppression had begun, God brought them out of Egypt "on the selfsame day," the record says.

God used Joseph, in Egypt, to predict accurately what would happen to the butler and the baker in three days. God also used Joseph to interpret Pharaoh's dream, which pointed forward to seven years of famine.

When the Israelites, at the border of the promised land, lacked faith to enter it, they were told that as the spies spent forty days in the land so the people must wander forty years in the wilderness, each day representing a literal year. They did.

The prophet Elijah told Ahab that there would be "neither dew nor rain in the next few years." The famine lasted three years and a half.

Do you see how precisely all these prophecies were fulfilled? When God's people repeatedly rebelled, they were permitted to be taken captive to Babylon. That captivity was to last seventy years. And when the time was up, God brought them back to their own land.

The prophet Daniel accurately predicted that the proud king of Babylon would be banished from his throne, and that his humiliating experience would continue for "seven times"—or seven literal years.

And now it becomes even more interesting. In a remarkable prophecy in the book of Daniel, God revealed that a probation period of seventy weeks, or 490 literal years, would be granted to the Jewish nation. (You recall that in symbolic prophecy a day represents a literal year. So seventy weeks would be 490 years.) At the end of the 490 years, in A.D. 34, the gospel began to be preached to the Gentiles—precisely fulfilling the prophecy.

That same prophecy of Daniel, even more remarkably, pinpointed the year that Jesus began His ministry—A.D. 27—and the year that he would be crucified—A.D. 31. You understand, of course, that we are getting only a quick overview of the prophecy here.

But now I want to ask you a question. Now that we see how amazingly and how precisely these time prophecies have been fulfilled, wouldn't you expect to find something in the Scriptures about when the world will end? Would God leave us in the dark about the most important event of all?

Now it is true that we are not told the exact time of our Lord's return. Jesus said, "No one knows about that day or hour, not even the angels in heaven, nor the Son, but only the Father." Matthew 24:36, NIV.

We cannot know the day and the hour. But Jesus Himself, as well as the Bible prophets, gave us many signs that would signal the nearness of His coming. They are being fulfilled before our eyes.

But is there no time prophecy that reaches down to these last days to let us know that they are indeed *the* last days?

Yes, there is. It is a prophecy so important, a time period so significant, that we find it mentioned seven times in the Bible— twice in the book of Daniel, and five times in the book of Revelation. The time period is given in three different ways— in prophetic days, in prophetic months, and in prophetic years. Twice it is given as 1260 days, twice as forty-two months, and three times as three years and a half. All of these refer to exactly the same period of time—1260 years. For you remember that in symbolic prophecy a day represents a literal year.

This 1260-year period, beginning in A.D. 538 and extending to 1798, corresponds roughly to the years of medieval persecution. And its close, the year 1798, marks the beginning of what Daniel calls "the time of the end."

Jesus spoke of this period of persecution. He said, "For then there will be great distress, unequaled from the beginning of the world until now—and never to be equaled again." Matthew 24:21, NIV. Yet merciful God that He is, He would not allow the distress, the persecution, to continue to the end of the time period. It would be cut short. "If those days had not been cut short, no one would survive, but for the sake of the elect those days will be shortened." Verse 22.

But now notice what would happen. Still reading from the prophecy of Jesus in Matthew 24, "Immediately after the distress of those days 'the sun will be darkened, and the moon will not give its light; the stars will fall from the sky, and the heavenly bodies will be shaken.'" Verse 29. The persecution ceased along about 1776, the year of the American Declaration of Independence. Four years later, on May 19, 1780, still within the time period but after the persecution, came New England's famous Dark Day. And the strange darkness of the day was followed by the equally strange darkness of the night, just as Jesus had said. And thousands got the message—that He would soon return. In fact, many thought the end of the world was already here—on that dark morning of May 19. Not many years later, on November 13, 1833, the prediction of Jesus that the stars would fall from the sky was fulfilled by the greatest meteor shower ever witnessed.

Do you see what we are doing? We are tracing the time prophecies down just as far as we can. We have discovered that the year 1798 marked the beginning of the end time. The last of these signs in the heavens took us to the year 1833. And now we can go only eleven years farther. And then that's all.

Eleven years farther. For the same prophecy of Daniel that pinpointed the year of the crucifixion, a prophecy that extends over 2300 years, the longest time prophecy in the Bible—that prophecy terminates in the year 1844. In previous telecast presentations we discovered that in the year 1844, Jesus began an investigation of the records of men—in preparation for His coming and the separation of the saved from the lost which must take place at that time. The year 1844. That's all there is. There is no specific time prophecy in the Bible that takes us any farther!

Do you see what this means? It means that so far as any time prophecy is concerned, Jesus could have returned to this earth any time after 1844. He is not waiting for any prophetic time period to end. No time prophecy is holding Him back. Then why hasn't He returned? For nearly two hundred years we have been living in the time of the end. Why isn't He here? Scripture provides the answer. "The Lord is not slow in keeping his promise, as some understand slowness. He is patient with you, not wanting anyone to perish, but everyone to come to repentance." 2 Peter 3:9, NIV.

Do you see the reason for the delay? Our wonderful Lord, our compassionate, loving Saviour, doesn't want anyone to be lost. And so He holds up the final flight of time, He slows the march of history—because some have not yet made a decision. And He doesn't want one to be lost!

Notice again the scripture that we read earlier. "After this I saw four angels standing at the four corners of the earth, holding back the four winds of the earth. . . . Then I saw another angel coming up from the east, having the seal of the living God. He called out in a loud voice to the four angels. . . : 'Do not harm the land or the sea or the trees until we put a seal on the foreheads of the servants of our God.' " Revelation 7:1-3, NIV.

And now you know why the winds of trouble and terror and all-out war have not yet been unleashed. Now you know why a lighted match in the Middle East has not blown us into World War III. Now you know why hurricanes so often have turned aside. Now you know why doomsday hasn't happened to an unsuspecting planet—yet.

But it will not always be this way. Today, as you read these words, the angels have not let go, though it seems that they must be loosening their grip. Today, as you read these words, it is not too late to make your choice for eternity. Today, as you read these words, I can tell you, on the authority of scripture, that Jesus will not return today. There are still some predicted events to be fulfilled.

But tomorrow the words that you read today may be out of date. The words that are true today may not be true tomorrow. For tomorrow the roar of unleashed winds may deafen us with their fury. And once they are unleashed, once time begins its final approach for a rendezvous with eternity, the climactic events referred to in the Book of Revelation, will be fulfilled with a rapidity that will take our breath away!

Are you ready for the winds to blow? Is there a mark on your forehead that no human eye can see—a mark that says you have chosen the Lord Jesus and want to be His forever?

If you haven't made that choice, you can make it now. Whoever you are, wherever you are, whatever you have done and however black your sins, you can make that choice now, and be forgiven, by asking the Lord Jesus to prepare you for that day, to wash you in His precious blood, and take your sins away.

Rescue From Orion

It was September 23, 1922. The old *U.S.S. Mississippi*, with a new name, lay at anchor in the harbor of Mitylene—an island in the Aegean Sea.

In the gray morning a young American civilian had come out to the ship in a borrowed rowboat and asked to see the captain. And now, twelve hours later, he had just delivered an ultimatum to the Greek government.

It happened this way. Not many weeks earlier a man named Asa Jennings, with his wife and family, had been sent by the Y.M.C.A. to the Turkish city of Smyrna. His assignment—to study what might be done to smooth relations between the Turks and Armenians and Greeks and Jews of that troubled city.

Things had happened fast. The Allies, you may recall, had given Smyrna to the Greeks as a reward for their participation in the war. The Greek army had moved into Smyrna and pushed inland toward Ankara. But Ataturk had rallied the Turkish people behind him in a daring drive for independence.

The Greek army was confident of victory. Its troups were pushing steadily toward the heart of the country—when suddenly they retreated before Ataturk. They burned and pillaged their way back to Smyrna.

The Greek troups, in their wild retreat, forced their own countrymen, as well as the Armenians, to abandon their homes and flee to the coast. Every road to the sea was choked with refugees. And then, believe it or not, the Greek soldiers, think-

181

ing only of their own safety, simply boarded ship and sailed away. The refugees were left to make out as best they could.

And then suddenly—no one seems to know just how—Smyrna was in flames. The great mass of refugees were pushed toward the sea, with the fire behind them.

Asa Jennings, while the city was still burning, put his little family aboard an American destroyer. But he stayed behind to see what he could do for the refugees. Somehow he arranged for food to be sent in. But this suffering mass of humanity that choked the quay, caught between fire and sea, needed more than food. They needed ships!

Now providentially, it seemed, the twenty Greek transports that had carried the Greek soldiers away to safety were anchored at Mitylene. So he lost no time in getting to Mitylene. Surely Greek ships would be willing to save Greek people. But General Frankos, in charge of the transports, was cautious and couldn't make up his mind.

It was then that Asa Jennings sighted the old *U.S.S. Mississippi* at anchor and rowed out through the early morning mist to board her. He was determined to go over the head of General Frankos and make contact directly with the Greek government in Athens.

He told his story to the captain. He then asked that a code message be sent to Athens, requesting that all ships in the waters about Smyrna be placed at his disposal. It was four o'clock in the morning.

A message came back, "Who are you?"

A natural question. He had been in that part of the world only about a month, and no one had ever heard of him.

He sent word back, "I am in charge of American relief at Mitylene." He did not explain that he was in charge only by virtue of being the only American there.

Athens outdid General Frankos in caution. The cabinet would have to decide. The cabinet was not in session. The cabinet would meet in the morning. What protection would be given the ships? Would American destroyers accompany them? Did that mean that American destroyers would protect the ships if the Turks should try to take them? And so it went.

Finally, at four in the afternoon, the young American's patience was exhausted. He wired Athens that if he did not receive a favorable reply by six o'clock, he would wire openly, without code—letting all the world know that the Greek government had refused to rescue its own people from certain death.

It worked. Shortly before six o'clock a message came through: ALL SHIPS IN AEGEAN PLACED YOUR COMMAND. REMOVE REFUGEES SMYRNA.

Those ten words meant life for many thousands. They also meant that a young, unknown American had just been made Admiral of the Greek navy!

And so he assumed command. The captains of the twenty ships were asked to be ready to leave for Smyrna by midnight. And then at midnight he ordered the Greek flag run down, an American flag flown in its place, with a signal that meant "Follow me." He mounted the bridge and ordered full steam ahead.

Picture the scene if you can. As the ships moved toward Smyrna, he could see from his station on the bridge the smoking ruins of what had once been the business section of town. Directly in front, gaunt brick and stone skeletons of once fine buildings pushed themselves up from the charred debris. And at the water's edge, stretching for miles, was what looked like a lifeless black border. Yet he knew that it was a border of living sufferers waiting, hoping, praying—as they had done every moment for days—for ships, ships, ships!

As the ships moved closer, and the shore spread out before him, it seemed as if every face on that quay was turned toward them, and every arm outstretched to bring them in. It seemed that the whole shore moved out to grasp them. The air was filled with the cries of those thousands—cries of such joy that the sound pierced to the very marrow of his bones. No need for anyone to tell them what those ships were for. They who had scanned that watery horizon for days looking wistfully for ships, did not have to be told that here was help, that here was life and safety!

Never had Asa Jennings been so thankful, so truly happy, as on that early morning when he realized that at last—and thank God in time—he had been able to bring hope, and a new life, to those despairing legions!

It was Asa Jennings' son who told me the story.

I can never forget it. Nor can I forget the striking parallel that I know will happen soon. A spectacular rescue—not from the sea, but from the sky. Involving not three hundred thousand refugees on a single shore, but—if only they would be willing—every man, woman, and child on a shaking, burning, convulsing planet, pushed to the brink—the brink of oblivion. And no way out but rescue from the sky!

It is difficult to say just when we first decided that this planet might become an undesirable neighborhood. It might have been the day that Hiroshima became the first casualty of the atomic age. Or it might have been before that—on the morning of our first atomic test at Los Alamos—when we got our first glimpse of what we were really handling.

Exodus Earth. Somewhere to go if the wrong man wins the election. Somewhere to go if some scheming dictator takes over. Somewhere to go if the bomb gets into the hands of madmen. Somewhere to go when the earth's food runs out, when its oil runs out, when its land runs out, when its air and its water and its dust are unsafe. Somewhere to go when the Lady of Liberty in New York Harbor can no longer offer peace and promise to the tired and the poor. And so we started reading up on stellar real estate. We started talking seriously about exodus Earth.

But could we escape in time? That was the question. We soon realized that other planets are far too distant. They could never be colonized in time to help this generation. So now we are talking about platforms in space—space colonies in our own earth orbit.

But even with these bold plans, will we escape in time? Or will we still be here when the Lord Jesus returns to this earth? Come with me to the book of Revelation. Here is described the moving scene that takes place as the Son of God appears in the turbulent skies: "The sky receded like a scroll, rolling up, and every mountain and island was removed from its place. Then the kings of the earth, the princes, the generals, the rich, the mighty, and every slave and every free man hid in caves and among the rocks of the mountains. They called to the mountains and the rocks, 'Fall on us and hide us from the face of him who sits on the throne and from the wrath of the Lamb! For the great day of their wrath has come, and who can stand?' " Revelation 6:14-17, NIV.

Evidently, when the Creator returns to this earth, He will not find that men, even the richest and the mightiest, have just slipped out the back door to the moon. They will not have perfected some emergency exit into outer space. They will be right here, still trapped on this planet, praying for the rocks and mountains to hide them from the face of the rejected Saviour!

Friend, I agree that exodus Earth will soon be imperative. There will come a day when frightened, frustrated, frantic men and women will call out in desperate seriousness—and it won't be from the Broadway stage—"Stop the world! I want to get off!"

But God has not been caught unprepared. He has His own exodus Earth. It will happen. And it will happen in time. I never tire of the way the Apostle Paul describes it: "The Lord himself shall descend from heaven with a shout, with the voice of the archangel, and with the trump of God: and the dead in Christ shall rise first: then we which are alive and remain shall be caught up together with them in the clouds, to meet the Lord in the air: and so shall we ever be with the Lord." 1 Thessalonians 4:16, 17, KJV.

News. Good news. Encouraging news. Comforting news. This isn't death. This is resurrection. This isn't destruction. This is survival. This isn't panic. This is rescue. Like the ships moving in to Smyrna. It's a way off this planet. And it's in time. Just in time!

This isn't gloom. This isn't doom. This isn't something to spoil your plans. This isn't something to fear—or dread—or wish you could postpone. That is, unless you don't want to be rescued. And who wouldn't want to be rescued in an hour like that?

Who would have chosen to turn back to the smoking ruins of Smyrna—with ships in sight? And who would want to turn back to this smoking, shaking, convulsing planet with rescue on the way?

Picture it if you can. Like the ships at Smyrna. A vast mass of humanity pushed to the edge of a smoking, ruined, convulsing world. Caught between the fires of time and the realities of eternity. Desperate for a way off this planet. Scanning the skies for the first hint that rescue is on the way. Staring into space. Straining our eyes for the first glimpse of our Lord as He emerges from the corridors of Orion and rides the cloud closer and closer to the earth!

Every face is turned toward the sky. Every eye filled with tears of irrepressible joy. Every voice shouting His welcome. Every arm outstretched to bring Him in. As if the earth itself reached out to grasp its Creator!

No need to tell us why He has come. We who have scanned the heavens wistfully for days, while a planet burns behind us, don't have to be told that here is rescue from the skies. We have waited for our Lord. And now at last He is here!

This is the escape into space that God has planned. Are you ready for it? Am I? Will you and I be aboard that living starship as it begins to move—on its return trip?

That space trip has been scheduled by God Himself. And it won't be canceled. It is sure. It is certain. The only question is this: Who will get to go?

David asks that question: "Who may ascend into the hill of the Lord? And who may stand in his holy place?" Psalm 24:3, NASB.

And back comes the answer: "He who has clean hands and a pure heart." Verse 4.

The cost? Just a surrendered heart. A heart cleansed. A heart changed. A proud, selfish heart made selfless and humble. A hard heart made kind. A heart that has been to Calvary—and will never be the same again. A heart made strong enough to stand in that tumultuous day!

Think about that day. Think about it over and over. Let it give you something to live for. Could anything be more exciting to contemplate? Seeing first a small black cloud in the eastern sky. You watch it move nearer and nearer till it becomes a glorious white. A cloud like none you've ever seen before. A cloud of angels—uncounted angels. Hearing a sound like none you've ever heard before. The sound of a trumpet echoing round the world. A voice like none you've ever heard before. The voice of the Lord Jesus. Calling the dead to life. The earth shaking. The tombs bursting open. Angels everywhere. Carrying little children, in the bloom of perfect health, from the broken graves. Placing them in their mothers' arms. Shouts of joy as loved ones long separated by death are reunited, never to part again!

And then, together with those happy, resurrected ones, we who have waited through the long night are caught up into that angel starship, ready for the trip home!

I like to try to picture that space vehicle. A cloud of shining angels. A cloud chariot with living wings on either side, and living wheels beneath. A rainbow above it, and the appearance of fire beneath. Jesus riding the cloud—and not a person missed who really wanted to make the trip. Ten thousand angels surrounding the cloud and singing the praise of their Creator. Moving up through the glittering, star-studded corridor of Orion. A living starship on the way to the City of God!

Will your name be on the passenger list? It can be. There's only one requirement. It's the word "pardon," written in the blood of the Lord Jesus Christ, beside your name!

The Whisper of the Ax

The earthiness of the sixties was more than a move back to nature. It was more than a concern for the environment, more than a rejection of materialism as a satisfactory goal in life. It was a parting of the ways with traditional morality. It was an embracing of permissiveness and situation ethics. It was an open and bold rejection of all absolutes in moral conduct.

But the permissiveness of the sixties was not to be the final chapter. It *could* not be. For if the predictions of the book of Revelation were to be fulfilled, there must come a change. There must be a moral backlash. Absolutes reminiscent of Puritan days would again be accepted—and an attempt would be made to force them upon others.

This is shaping up now. Permissiveness has had its day, and it hasn't worked. We are living in the backlash. It is apparent now that society, if it is to survive, if anything is to be done about the accelerating lawlessness that threatens us all, simply must have some absolutes. And the pendulum has swung so far to the right that there is talk of legislating morality—and permitting no deviation from the beliefs of whatever group may be in the driver's seat.

But trying to legislate morality doesn't work. It never has—and never will. The marriage of strong legislation with the weakness of human nature may produce the appearance of strength. The outward conduct may be changed. But the heart is not changed. And God says the heart is desperately wicked. See Jeremiah 17:9.

189

You can force a man not to swear in public—or punish him if he does—but that doesn't clean up his thoughts. You can force a child to listen to Bible reading and prayers in the school. But you cannot force him either to believe or to pray. You can force a family to go to church, but you cannot make them have a personal relationship with God. You can shoot a man and quite effectively stop his thinking. But so long as he lives you cannot make him think what you want him to think!

Yet more and more, according to the book of Revelation, we shall see the attempt to cure our moral deterioration with force. Coercion will soon be no stranger.

Even in the area of politics and government there is a growing dissatisfaction with what is seen as weakness. There is an increasing demand for tough talk and tough action. It is becoming easier to understand how a nation represented in Revelation 13 as having the characteristics of a lamb, could yet speak as a dragon—even in the area of morals, with church and state uniting to restrict the personal liberty once considered sacred to all.

Partly strong and partly weak: that is the prophet Daniel's description of our society. See Daniel 2:41, 42. Strong in military power, strong enough to split the atom. Strong enough to speak as a dragon. Yet so weak in moral power that the might of the state is called in to do what the church cannot!

Will it happen? Certainly it will. God's Word has never failed!

But it will happen only as Christians disregard the clear counsel of the Lord they profess to worship. For Jesus said, "Render therefore unto Caesar the things which are Caesar's; and unto God the things that are God's." Matthew 22:21, KJV.

Those words of Jesus erect a barrier between church and state that we tamper with at our own risk. But that barrier is crumbling—and crumbling fast!

The change that we see today would have seemed impossible in the sixties, but it is happening. Permissiveness is giving way to movements that are antigay, antiabortion, antitax, and pro capital punishment.

I need not tell you that radio talk shows are one indication of the pulse of the people—of their reaction on current issues. One evening on a San Francisco talk show, a gentleman called in. I don't recall what had happened to trigger the discussion. But this, in substance, is what he said: "God is not going to tolerate baby killing and homosexuality. And He isn't going to tolerate us if we tolerate them." Then he continued, "Now we'll forget the past because you didn't know better. But if it continues—I'm going to be ready with my gun!"

Now you would expect that such a comment would either be passed off as a crank call or that it would stir up a flood of protest calls from other listeners. But nothing like that happened. The discussion continued. And the frightening thing is that the actual *execution* of moral offenders was *not* discussed as an impossible option. I didn't hear a single voice protest that such a thing was unthinkable in a land like ours. Rather, the actual extermination of people who deviate from Bible morality, as interpreted by the mood of society, was considered at least something to discuss!

A few years back homosexuality was more or less accepted as simply a preference of lifestyle. Now suddenly it was a sin not to be tolerated—with death as a possible punishment!

Now certainly it would be an ideal situation if everybody would live according to Bible standards of morality. And I am not forgetting that the ancient city of Sodom was destroyed with fire and brimstone for its moral deviation. It ought to make us nervous when one of our large cities welcomes and even honors those guilty of the same sin. But it was God who decided the fate of Sodom. I don't think we are qualified to play God!

It would be a wonderful thing, I say, if everyone would live according to the Bible. But *whose interpretation of the Bible?* That is the question!

Two guests were appearing on national television. They were asked, "Why should *your* policies be enforced on the American people?" and one of the guests boomed out, "Because one of us is right. And the other is wrong!"

And some of the causes being espoused by Christians today are not moral issues at all. They are purely political—in some cases little more than personal opinion.

Human nature finds it easy to make a moral issue out of a personal preference. I was told of a woman who considered it morally wrong to wear perfume—except the brand she used. We can hope legislation doesn't come to that!

The name of the game is power. Are we fast approaching the day when prophets will carry guns and the will of God will be interpreted by rifle? Or have we already entered it?

More and more of the world's political confrontations have religious overtones. It took only a band of angry Iranian students to plunge us into a frightening awareness of Moslem power. Afghanistan climbed out of the map and into common talk in one day. Ireland as an arena of religious conflict is no longer unique. Enemies, too often, are enemies simply because of their religion or lack of religion.

To the tribal mind of Afghanistan, communism means godlessness. "You have a book, we have a book," the Afghans will say to Christian visitors—referring to the Bible and the Koran. "But Russians—no book!"

Jesus said to His disciples, "A time is coming when anyone who kills you will think he is offering a service to God." John 16:2, NIV.

Is it possible that those words of Jesus will be fulfilled again in our day?

There are many factors, many attitudes and trends emerging today, that could move us easily into a marriage of church and state and a loss of our cherished freedoms.

Ever since Jonestown there has been a critical awareness of the cults—and a call for both investigation and legislation of their activities. Legislators have held back for fear of violating the church-state barrier. But could one more disaster, one more Jonestown, tip the balance?

And what if the people, outraged by some tragedy, take the situation into their own hands? Already, in one city, residents banded together and attempted to drive a cult out of town!

How long will it be until your church or mine is labeled a cult, your belief or mine considered strange or odd and therefore a threat to society?

The right to differ, whether a man is right or wrong, is a sa-

cred legacy that must be defended at all costs. But unfortunately, sometimes the most ardent and intelligent defenders of
political liberty are the first to put chains on religious freedom.
Molly Anderson Haley said it so well:

> Across the way my neighbor's windows shine.
>   His roof-tree shields him from the storms that frown.
>   He toiled and saved to built it, staunch and brown.
> And though my neighbor's house is not like mine,
>   I would not pull it down!
>
> With patient care my neighbor, too, had built
>   A house of faith, wherein his soul might stay,
>   A haven from the winds that sweep life's way.
> It differed from my own—I feel no guilt—
>   I burned it yesterday!

What strange reasoning, what manipulation of logic, leads
men and nations to honor men's civil rights—but scorn their
right to worship as they choose? Or not to worship at all? Yet
that is the kind of intolerance that has painted crimson the
pages of history!

And it will happen again—if we are to believe the book of
Revelation.

A few decades ago, many a mind rejected the predictions of
Revelation 13. They seemed too impossible. Bigotry—religious
persecution—in a nation founded on the principles of freedom?
Never! It just couldn't happen!

But now—almost overnight, it seems—the calm and compla-
cency is shattered by the not-too-distant clank of the chain.
Erupting before our unbelieving eyes are movements, full-
grown at birth, that could rapidly turn our cherished personal
liberties into souvenirs of a past that has slipped away. The
rumblings of Revelation have become a mighty crescendo in a
symphony about to be finished. Already creeping into the thinking of this generation is the disturbing and ominous idea that
those who won't go along with the religious views and practices of
those in power, perhaps—just perhaps—ought to be eliminated!

Bigotry is surfacing like white fins in the surf. And if we aren't disturbed, we ought to be!

Yet all the while we witness a welcome return to morality. We seem to have entered some sort of religious revival. The backlash against the permissiveness of the sixties is real, and it makes us feel more secure. And some are praying that the bandwagon of moral concern doesn't miss Washington. For God knows how much that city on the Potomac needs it! But that is where the issues become delicate. Speak out against the evils of our day—yes. Legislate—no.

In recent years we have witnessed a tremendous upsurge of fundamentalism in the United States. We have also witnessed it, again and again, in Moslem lands. We have stood aghast as we have seen, in countries far from our shores, the harsh punishment, the actual execution of moral offenders—and heard it defended as simply following the Koran!

We have thanked God that it couldn't happen here. But are we sure? Some of history's worst atrocities have been committed in the name of religion. There is no persecution so cruel as religious persecution. There is no terror so ruthless as terror in the name of God!

Is this what the book of Revelation is predicting?

Open your Bible, if you will, to the thirteenth chapter of Revelation. Look at it carefully, for it is extremely significant for our time.

Verse one. We see here a beast—the symbol of a nation, a kingdom, a power. In this instance it must be a combination of both political and religious power, for crowns suggest political power, and blasphemy an involvement in religion.

Verse two. The beast receives his power, his headquarters, and his authority directly or indirectly from the dragon, who is Satan.

Verses three and four. The beast receives worship that is virtually universal. And Satan also is worshiped—at least indirectly.

Verse five to seven. Blasphemy again is emphasized. This beast is attempting to exercise power that belongs only to God. It is a persecuting power, evidently the same power mentioned in Daniel 7:25, where it is described as persecuting the saints and attempting to change God's law. Its power would extend over a period of 1260 years—a day in prophecy representing a literal year. This same period of persecution is described in Revelation 12:6, 14.

Verse eight. We can expect the whole world to worship the beast—except for those whose names are written in the Lamb's book of life.

Verse eleven. Here we see another beast, emerging at a later time. This is a lamblike symbol representing a nation professing to be Christlike and freedom loving, but which changes character and eventually speaks as a dragon. That is, it manifests the attributes of Satan. The symbols could also indicate that it begins as a Christian nation but later espouses the propaganda of the dragon—spiritualism.

Verse twelve. This second beast eventually, like the first beast, becomes a combination of religious and political power, for it causes the whole world to worship the first beast. And worship, of course, is a function of religion, not politics. Notice also that the first beast has suffered a severe wound, but has recovered.

Verse thirteen. This second beast is a miracle-working power, even bringing fire down from heaven. Again this suggests an involvement with spiritualism, the power of Satan.

Verse fourteen. By these miracles, counterfeit miracles, this second beast deceives the whole world and persuades the people to create an image of the first beast. When this image is formed, when a combination of religious and political power similar to that of the first beast has been created, then the second beast has forever abandoned its lamblike beginning, its Christian principles, and itself becomes a persecuting power!

It is significant also, in this verse, that a democracy or democracies must be involved. The image of the beast is not something imposed upon men by a dictator or monarch against their will. *It is the people who do it.* Notice the wording—"saying to them that dwell on the earth, that *they* should make an image to the beast." KJV.

Verse fifteen. The image of the beast, with power granted by the people, decrees death to all who refuse to worship the image of the beast. Here is what we have feared, what we have thought could never happen—legislation that would provide for the extermination of those who refuse to go along with the religious practices of the majority—or of those in power.

Verse sixteen. A mark is urged upon all—as a sign of allegiance to the beast and its image.

Verse seventeen. Those who refuse to receive the mark are not permitted to buy or sell.

Something very strange is predicted here—a Christian people, zealous for the morality of their neighbors, adopting the philosophies and methods of the dragon to bring it about. And it is the people—not the antichrist or the beast or the image of the beast or the dragon himself, though all these are the persuading influence—*it is the people who do it!*

It would seem that any threat to religious freedom would come from the non-Christian world. We expect it from atheistic dictators. But suddenly the threat seems to be coming not from the unbelieving world, but from a Christian element that in its zeal would like to use the power of the state to impose its own version of morality, its own interpretations of Scripture, along with its own political views, upon the nation and the world!

American presidents have been fond of praising the American people and expressing great confidence in them. Jimmy Carter was one whose speeches were liberally sprinkled with the expression, "the American people." He was confident the American people would understand this or that, would do this or that, would not permit this or that. And he was no exception. We have been educated to believe that the people are always right, that the majority should rule, that democracy is sacred. And certainly no better form of government is available on this planet—now.

But just as a monarchy is no better than its king, a dictatorship no better than its dictator, just so a democracy is no better than its people. The pulse of the people is not always a safe guide. If the heart is not right, the pulse will not be right!

It is difficult to see how a freedom-loving people could ever turn to force and coercion. But who knows what the response of the people night be, for instance, if the nation's economy should collapse? Is it possible that citizens might be willing to sacrifice some of their freedoms in exchange for relief from their economic problems? Is it possible that the majority would be willing to accept a measure of regimentation, a loss of some of their liberty, so long as their personal life-style was not seriously affected?

The people, in a severe economic crisis, would likely accept as a leader most anyone who would promise a way out. An aspiring antichrist would find them easy prey, delightfully vulnerable to his promises and propaganda!

Wouldn't it be a tragedy to step into an erupting fulfillment of Revelation—unprepared?

A citizen who was present at the execution of Marie-Antoinette, in the year 1793, said of the experience: "I was sitting so close I could hear the whisper of the ax!"

Friend, above the din of confused and quarreling voices, above the roar of jets overhead, above the hypnotic beat of rock and the booming of distant cannons and the clatter of jackhammers in the street—above it all, if you listen closely, you too can hear *the whisper of the ax!*

Forever Marked

"When I use a word, it means just what I choose it to mean, neither more nor less." Humpty-Dumpty was speaking—in *Alice in Wonderland*. But we still live in an unpredictable wonderland where words mean different things to different people. And some words, such as *love* and *loyalty* and *obedience*, have had a real workout. It seems they can be stretched—or shrunk—to mean most anything.

But a certain farmer, in a story told by Steve Dickerson seemed to have the right idea. It goes like this:

Bill grew up on a farm. And there was never any question about his future. He would be a farmer like his dad.

He went to college and studied agriculture. That gave him the scientific know-how. But where would he get the money to buy a farm?

One day his father said, "Bill, I'm getting old. I'm almost ready to retire. I'd like to give the farm to you."

Bill was speechless. His problem was solved!

But the older man went on. "There's just one stipulation. I want you to run the farm strictly according to my directions for the first year. After that, it's yours."

That was fair enough. Dad was a good farmer. He knew what he was doing. And just think—after a year the farm would be his!

The two men spent the next few days going from field to field. Bill carried a notebook and wrote down just what his father wanted him to plant in each field. Then his father and mother left for a vacation.

Bill was curious. It would be interesting to see how his father's directions checked out with what he had learned at college. He got out his soil-testing kit and started around the farm again. As he went from one field to another, he was impressed with his father's wisdom. In each field his dad had scooped up a handful of soil and examined it carefully before deciding what to plant. And he had been right every time. Every time he had chosen the very crop that, according to what Bill had learned in college, would grow best in that particular soil!

Every time, until Bill came to the last field. His father had said to plant corn, but he must have made a mistake. The soil appeared to be sandy and poor. Plant corn! Why, Bill was sure that the slightest wind would tear the plants right out of the soil. And even if the stalks weren't blown over, he was sure that the corn would be sickly. Dad must have made a mistake.

Bill's analysis showed that the soil would be perfect for peanuts. Dad would want every crop to be a success. He would be pleased to see that all the money spent on Bill's education had paid off. So Bill planted peanuts.

Dad came back at harvesttime. He said the farm had never looked so good. Bill took him around and showed him the wheat and the potatoes and the alfalfa.

"But where's the corn?" Dad wanted to know. "I thought I told you to plant corn."

Bill said, "Well, yes, Dad. That was in this field over here. I went back and tested the soil in all the fields. You were exactly right in all except this one, so I thought you must have made a mistake. I was sure you would rather see a good crop of peanuts than a sickly crop of corn."

Dad shook his head sadly. "Bill," he said, "you haven't followed my directions in any of these fields. You've followed your own judgment in every case. It just happened you agreed with me in all points except one. But as soon as there was any question, you did what you thought best in spite of what I had directed you to do. I'm sorry, Bill, but you'll have to look elsewhere for a farm of your own."

How about it? Was Bill's father too harsh? Or was he absolutely right? Does it mean anything at all to follow directions—

especially when they are God's directions—only when we happen to agree with them?

Most of us are not farmers. But our Father—like Bill's dad—has written down on slabs of stone, some specific directions for us. And on condition that we follow them, He promises not a farm, but a future beyond our wildest dreams—and never-ending life. We call those directions the Ten Commandments.

But millions today have brought out their own personal analyzing kits. They think it would be interesting to see how God's directions compare with what they've been taught at the university—or with their own philosophy of life and right and wrong. And what happens?

Millions today are improvising their own off-the-cuff morality to meet their moods. They have decided that God's directions are outdated and certainly not relevant for this "enlightened" generation. And even if they agree with God part of the time, they are sure that in some instances He made a mistake—or just didn't mean what He said. And so they are planting peanuts—and thinking how pleased God will be when He sees the crop!

Millions actually believe that God sometimes throws His Ten Commandments into reverse. They think it is all right to steal in an emergency. Or lie if it will keep you out of jail. Or commit adultery if, as Joseph Fletcher has suggested, having a child is the only way to get out of a concentration camp. Millions today follow God's directions when they agree with them—and ignore them when they don't seem to make sense.

But if we obey only when we agree, have we obeyed at all?

Jesus said, "Not everyone who says to me, 'Lord, Lord,' will enter the kingdom of heaven, but only he who does the will of my Father who is in heaven." Matthew 7:21, NIV.

Are we in danger of losing a fabulous future the way Bill lost a farm?

You see, God has the same problem today that He had with our first parents. He wanted to give them never-ending life, but He dared not give them immortality without first testing their loyalty. He must be sure that they could be trusted with a life that never ends!

How could He do this? What sort of test could He devise that would give Him absolute assurance of their loyalty—or tragic proof that they could not be trusted with the gift He wanted to give them? Promises were not enough. Promises are easy to make.

God could have put an active volcano, a crater of fire, on the edge of the Garden. He could have told Adam and Eve that to jump into it would mean death. And they would undoubtedly have stayed away from it for sure. No man in his right mind is going to jump into a seething caldera when the heat of it, even at a safe distance, burns the whiskers off his face!

No! God must devise a test that, to human reasoning, seemed not to make sense. Obedience must stem from loyalty alone—nothing else!

Let me illustrate. The story is told of a railroad worker who lived near the tracks. He was off duty that day. He looked up from his work in the yard to see his little boy, four and a half, playing on the tracks. And a train was thundering toward him!

There was no time to reach him and snatch him away. He called, but Johnny did not hear. Then he called out at the top of his voice, for there was time for nothing else, "Johnny, lie down and don't move!"

Johnny obeyed instantly and without even turning to look his father's way. The train rushed over the motionless boy. And after the caboose had passed, the father gathered him up, his little heart pounding—but safe!

There was nothing in Johnny's short experience, his few short years, to qualify him to understand his father's strange command. But he didn't question it. He didn't ask why. He didn't delay. His father had spoken. And that was enough for him!

Just so, in Adam and Eve's experience there was nothing to qualify them to understand God's strange command. Why should the fruit of one tree, apparently just as beautiful, and as much to be desired as the others, have death within it? They didn't understand that the seemingly unimportant act of eating the fruit clearly revealed the weakness of their loyalty!

Now God, I say, has the same problem today that He had in

the Garden of Eden. Millions have professed loyalty to God. But obviously not all could be trusted with never-ending life. How else can their loyalty be tested—except with a command that makes no sense to the human mind?

Now we are ready to turn to the book of Revelation. You recall that in the thirteenth chapter there are some very frightening predictions. A *beast*—representing a kingdom, a nation, a power. In this case it is evidently a coalition of religious and political power. A *second beast*—a nation with lamblike characteristics at the beginning, but later speaking as a dragon. This *second beast*, evidently a democracy, persuades the people to create *an image of the first beast*—a similar coalition of religious and political power. This *image*, this coalition, pronounces *a death sentence* upon all who refuse to worship the *first beast*. And those who refuse to receive the *mark of the beast* are not permitted to *buy or sell*. Frightening, you will agree.

But in the *fourteenth* chapter, the next chapter, symbolized by three angels, each with a message, we find God's last call to men (verses 6-12). And in the message of the third angel (verses 9-11) we find the most fearful warning in all of the Scriptures— a warning against worshiping the beast and his image or receiving his mark!

Now this is not something to play games with. This is serious business. It appears to be death-if-you-do and death-if-you-don't. And no middle ground!

I am aware of the widespread notion that the book of Revelation can't be understood. But I ask you, Would God include so fearful a warning in His last call to men—if He knew that the identity of the beast and the nature of his mark could not be understood?

But before we explore some clues as to what the mark might be, what about God? Does God have a mark too? Yes, He does. And could it be that in the final confrontation, in the still ongoing controversy in which every one of us will be involved, whether we want to be or not—could it be that the choice will be between two marks, with our choice revealing our loyalty either to Christ or to the fallen angel? Yes, it will be exactly that. And I believe that if we understand the nature of God's mark, it will be easier to understand the nature of Satan's mark.

The idea of God placing a mark upon His people is not new. You recall that in ancient Egypt, on that fateful night when the destroying angel was to pass through the land, every Hebrew householder was to slay a lamb and place some of its blood on the doorpost. The destroying angel, seeing that mark, that identification, would spare that home.

Then in the ninth chapter of Ezekiel, we find a symbolic vision that was shown to the prophet. Israel, in its idolatry, had reached the point where punishment could no longer be delayed. And in this vision Ezekiel saw six men with weapons of slaughter. One of them, however, had a writer's inkhorn— probably a case containing pens, a knife, and ink. He was commanded to go through Jerusalem, preceding the others, and place a mark upon the foreheads of those individuals who were sighing and crying in their concern over the depravity of God's professed people. Then the other five men were to follow him through the city, sparing only those who had the mark upon their foreheads.

Keep in mind that this was a symbolic vision. Israel's punishment would not be executed by six men, and there was no literal mark. The punishment, when God removed His restraining hand, would come from the Chaldean armies. This was the primary fulfillment of what the prophet saw in vision. A secondary fulfillment will take place down in the last days.

In the seventh chapter of Revelation we see four angels holding the winds of war and strife. They are commissioned not to let them blow in full force upon the earth until the servants of God are sealed, or marked, in their foreheads.

What will this mark be? What test will God administer to His professed people that will reveal, once for all, who is safe to take into His kingdom and who is not, who can be trusted with never-ending life and who cannot? It must be something that has no foundation in human reason, something that doesn't seem to make sense, a command that His true people will obey simply because He has spoken. Like Johnny on the railroad track—obeying without asking why. That's the kind of test to look for.

We find a number of clues. All through the Scriptures the fact that God is the Creator is held out as distinguishing Him from false gods who never created anything. And I need not tell you that God's creatorship is under attack today. From the beginning the fact that Jesus created this earth has been a focal point of Satan's jealousy. And in God's last call to men we are urged to worship Him who made heaven and earth (Revelation 14:6, 7)—again suggesting that the matter of God's creatorship is a key issue in the final conflict.

In the last verse of Revelation 12 we see Satan angry with the people of God, going to war against them because they persist in keeping God's commandments. And in Daniel's prophecy (Daniel 7:25) we see a persecuting power, evidently the same as the first beast of Revelation 13, attempting to make some change in God's law. The apostle Paul (2 Thessalonians 2: 3, 4) describes the man of sin, the antichrist, as sitting in the temple of God and claiming that he *is* God.

God's authority, God's creatorship, God's commandments—these are the issues. And, as a test of loyalty, we can expect to find a command of God that seems not to be based on human reasoning.

With these clues in mind, scan with me the Ten Commandments, found in Exodus 20:3-17. The first three seem reasonable enough. If God is the true God, certainly we should not have any other gods or bow down to images of wood or stone. And certainly God should have our respect. The last six commandments are so reasonable that for thousands of years they have frequently been incorporated into the laws of nations—even nations that do not worship the true God.

But one commandment—the fourth—is different. It doesn't fit into man's reasoning. There seems to be no moral principle involved. It seems arbitrary. And in a sense it is. Our year is marked off by the journey of our planet around the sun. Our month is marked off by the recurrent phases of the moon, and our day by the rotation of the earth. But our week has no basis in the movements of heavenly bodies. This weekly cycle is marked off only by the Sabbath.

The commandment would not be so troublesome if it simply

asked for one day in seven as a day of rest. Most anyone would go along with the idea of a day off every seven days. Labor unions like it. Atheists like it. It certainly would not indicate any particular loyalty to God to take one day in seven for rest.

But the commandment specifies *the seventh* day. It is this specificity that makes it a problem, and often makes it inconvenient. Certainly the days are all alike, twenty-four hours long. What difference does it make which day we devote to rest and worship? It doesn't seem reasonable that God should specify a particular day. But He has. And there will always be those who love Him enough to obey without asking why!

Could this be the test we are looking for, a command that doesn't make sense to the human mind? It certainly fits. God, seemingly without reason, placed one tree in the center of the garden and declared it off limits to our first parents. Could it be that God has placed in the center of His law a command that doesn't answer easily to human reason—and that in these final days He will use it to measure the loyalty of every man, every woman, every child who professes to worship Him?

Yes, the Sabbath commandment is unique among the ten. There is no controversy about the other nine. Most any good citizen, Christian or not, will go along with them because they seem reasonable. But does any man, regardless of how often he goes to church or how much he puts in the offering plate or how spotless his moral character may be—does any man really obey God at all if he obeys only when he understands why, when he can see a reason, when he happens to agree with God, when a command makes sense? No, he doesn't. Like the farmer's son, he is really following his own judgment all the way!

Now I know that the identity of the day of rest may seem like a trivial matter. Surely, you say, there must be more important issues than quibbling about a day.

But we cannot always choose our challenges. The fireman cannot choose the location of the fires he fights. The soldier cannot choose where he will go to war. The lesson of the Falklands, for Britain, was this—battles will not always be fought where they seem most likely.

Ted Koppel, hosting ABC's "Viewpoint" program before a

live audience, was asked why the press at that time did not give more time to Africa. Why did newsmen give so much time to the Middle East and not Africa? The answer, of course, is that the news goes where the fire is, where the war is, where an enemy has chosen to attack. Vietnam was an obscure place to many Americans, but that's where the challenge was. Iran was not at the top of our priority list, but that's where our hostages were held. The North Pole would have made the headlines if our hostages had been there!

Satan is angry with the people who persist in obeying God's commands. See Revelation 12:17. The prophet Daniel predicted that an attempt would be made to change God's law. See Daniel 7:25. Then I ask you, Will Satan focus his attack on the commandments that men find reasonable and about which there is no controversy? Or will he zero in on the one which doesn't answer to human reason, the one which rests on God's authority alone? Wouldn't you expect the fallen angel to target especially the one that continually reminds men of their Creator? Of course!

Do you begin to see what the mark of God might be—and what the mark of the beast might be? If God uses the Sabbath commandment as a test of loyalty and if a faithful observance of that command marks a man as one who can be trusted to go God's way forever—then what might be the mark of the rebel camp? Could it be a substitute Sabbath, brought in from paganism during the dark ages when the Scriptures were not available to the people, a day of worship that rests, not on divine authority but on human authority? What could be more logical?

You see, the controversy isn't over a day at all. It's over authority. Whose authority will you accept? Will you accept the authority of God, or the authority of the beast as an agent of Satan? It matters not how trivial the command might appear. If God should say to you, "Go stand in the corner," and Satan should say, "Don't stand in the corner," it would probably seem downright ridiculous. But it would make a mighty big difference which command you obey, for it would mark you as a loyal follower of one or the other!

No one has the mark of the beast today. God will not permit any man to receive that mark until the issues are out in the open and every individual knows what he is doing. But when the issues are fully understood and he recognizes the critical and final nature of the step he is taking—*then*, if he deliberately chooses to obey a command of men in place of a command of God, if he yields to coercion and takes the easy way out when the going gets rough, he will have *marked himself*, by his action, as one no longer loyal to his God. The mark will be there. *In his forehead* if he believes the propaganda of Satan. *In his hand* if he knows it is false, but goes along with it anyway, because he can't take the pressure and ridicule of the crowd. The mark will be invisible to men. But angels will see it—and know where his loyalty lies!

And what of the mark of God? Even now our attitude toward the commandments of God may decide our destiny. But at this moment it has not become the crucial test of loyalty that it will be in the days ahead. There are still too many people outwardly faithful to the commands of God, including the Sabbath, whose commitment is only for fair weather. When the predictions of Revelation 13 become a reality, when it is no longer convenient to obey God, the superficial hangers-on will be shaken out. And those who keep the faith, even when it is a matter of life or death, will be giving God evidence that they can be trusted with never-ending life. The mark of God will be in their foreheads. His mark is never received in the hand, for God accepts only that worship which comes from the heart and mind. Satan, on the contrary, doesn't care how he gets his worship. If he cannot get it by choice, he will gladly accept it by force!

The mark of God. And the mark of the enemy. On the one hand a command that is based solely upon the authority of God. On the other hand a command that is based solely on the authority of men. This is the choice that is racing toward us!

Have we been weaving here a fabric of guesswork? Has there really been an attempt to change God's law? Is the challenge of God's authority about to surface openly and burst into flame? Yes. Daniel predicted it. Paul said it would come. Revelation spotlights it. And the power represented by the beast of Revela-

tion 13 comes along and says in substance, "Yes, we did it.
We're proud of it. We consider the act a mark of our authority." *

We are moving rapidly toward the day of final choices. And
we are preparing for that day by the little decisions, the seemingly insignificant choices we make along the way. If in these
little situations, we habitually choose the easy way—the popular way, we shall find it only natural, in the crisis, to decide the
same way—along with the crowd!

We shall have some surprises when we see who is strong—
and who is weak. Some that we thought were strong will prove
miserably weak. And some that we thought were weak will dis-
play the courage of David—and be forever marked as friends of
God!

Professor Wise—we shall call him that—was no friend of
God. And everybody in his five-hundred-member class knew it.
In September he had told them, "During the course of this se-
mester all who have the desire to remain in this section of An-
thropology 201 will learn the truth. In learning this truth you
will find every belief you have ever held about God or religion
in general will be destroyed." And in the weeks that followed he
had never missed an opportunity to criticize and ridicule religion.

And now the class was meeting for the last time before Christmas vacation. Dr. Wise was giving his annual lecture "proving"
that prayer is a fallacy. He had been giving this lecture for ten
years, so he knew it well. It had gone off so well the first time,
and was such hilarious entertainment, that he had made it an
annual event.

This day, as he finished his mocking attack, he stood up. He
was wearing what he always wore for this performance—jeans,
sneakers, and a T-shirt that read, "Jesus is coming again, and
boy, is He peeved."

He glared at the auditorium full of students and defiantly
inquired, "After two months in this class, is there anybody here

* The publishers of this book will be happy to refer you to detailed
evidence of what happened and the claims made by those involved. My
own book, *A Day to Remember*, would be helpful.

who still believes in the ridiculous notion of religion?"

He walked around to the front of his desk and stood gloating. In his upraised right hand he held a new piece of chalk. The classroom had a concrete floor. All eyes were glued on the professor. There was utter silence.

Then, with a mocking jeer, he went on with the challenge he had long since memorized: "Well, if there's anyone in this classroom who still believes in religion and the so-called power of prayer, I ask you to stand up and pray. Pray that when I drop this piece of chalk from my hand it will not break. . . . I defy you and this so-called power by stating this: 'Nothing—not all your prayers, not all your religion, not even your so-called God Himself, can stop this piece of chalk from breaking when I drop it.' I defy you to prove me wrong!"

There was a slight movement near the right side of the auditorium. Every eye turned. A boy named David stood up and walked to the aisle. Then he moved toward the front and stopped in front of his instructor. "Dr. Wise," he said in clear and confident tones, "I do."

"Well, how about this? We've here before us a real, live person who claims he believes in the stupid notion that God can answer his prayer. Is that right?"

"Yes, sir. I know God will answer my prayer."

"How about this?" the professor repeated. "But I tell you what. Just in case you misunderstood, I'll explain to you again exactly what I am going to do."

Then he went through the sequence again—how he would drop the chalk, it would shatter into a dozen fragments, and no power in the universe could keep it from shattering. Then he chided, "Do you still want to pray?"

"Yes, Professor, I sure do."

The professor reveled in this glorious moment of victory, gloating over what was about to happen. "Isn't this something? All right, class. I want you all to be real quiet and reverent-like while this boy prays." There was sarcasm in every word. Then he turned back to David. "Are you ready?"

And David replied, "Professor, I have been preparing for this moment all my life."

"All right, then. We'll all be real quiet and bow our heads while you pray." Never were words more mocking and derisive.

Not one of the more than five hundred could take their eyes off David. They all held their breath. The boy just turned his face heavenward and prayed, "God, I know You are real, and I pray in the name of and for the glory and honor of Your Son Jesus. And I pray for myself, who trusts You with all my heart. If it be Your will, do not let this piece of chalk break. Amen."

The sneering smile was still on the professor's face. "Is that it?"

David breathed a quiet "Yes."

Dr. Wise grasped the chalk in his right hand and held it up above his head in defiance. Then he let it fall. But that day a miracle happened. As the chalk tumbled toward the floor it fell against the leg of his jeans. Then it toppled down onto his canvas sneakers, and with a muffled tinkle it rolled to a stop on the concrete floor, unbroken!

The silence was deafening! Then a student burst into laughter. Soon another joined. In seconds the entire auditorium was laughing at the red-faced professor. Someone in the back of the auditorium shouted at the top of his voice, "You did it, David!" He turned and smiled—a careful, humble sort of smile. Then he just pointed upward. And everyone understood. Even the professor!

This David was not strong and muscular like the boy who herded sheep and killed a lion and a bear and a giant on the way to becoming king. This David was slight of stature and a little scrawny. He looked as if a little wind could blow him away. But scrawny little David had decided that such defiance of God could not be ignored. This modern Goliath must be challenged. And after all, his name was David! *

God hides the stuff of heroes in a thousand unsuspected places. And crisis always finds it. It will again!

* Used by permission of the author.

God's Yellow Ribbons

Victims of kidnapping are sometimes told that family and friends have forsaken them. And sometimes they are brainwashed into believing it.

How could we let fifty-two American hostages know that their country had not abandoned them?

Someone tied a yellow ribbon around an old oak tree—and yellow ribbons spread like the measles. But how would *the hostages* know? How would *they* know that eight brave men had lost their lives in an attempt to rescue them? How would *they* know that we were numbering our days by the days of their captivity? How *could* they know when bags full of mail addressed to them were left unopened—and when the few letters that were delivered were first carefully censored?

But love has a way of getting through. Militant students overlooked the value of a Valentine—in August—from a little girl. It said simply, "It's just not America without you!" And another, from a child in school, slipped past the censors. It said, "I'm awfully sorry they didn't get you out. I hope they try again."

Then there was a *Time* magazine which carried the full story of the rescue attempt. The story had been carefully removed—and then inadvertently stuffed into the back of the magazine and forgotten.

At Christmas time a visiting clergyman gave Morehead Kennedy the assurance he needed in one short sentence: "Nobody's talking about anything else!"

The fifty-two were not forgotten!

213

And then, on January 20, almost as abruptly as it had begun, the long ordeal was over. The fear and the hunger, the blindfolds and the isolation and the beatings, the terrible loneliness, the fake firing squads—all slipped into the past, to scar only their memories.

Four hundred and forty-four dull, dragging, seemingly endless days suddenly gave way to a tumult of joy and reunion and welcome that couldn't happen except in a dream. Yet it *was* happening—happening to fifty-two Americans who in their hours of darkness had been tempted to think nobody cared. It would take a while to sort it all out and be convinced that it was real!

Telephones! Milk to drink! No blindfolds! Moving about without asking permission! German children singing to make up for the Christmases they had missed! The Statue of Liberty lighted for the first time since 1976! Kissing American soil! Church bells ringing! Falling at last into the arms of loved ones! The memories were theirs to keep!

And each day brought more pictures to hang in memory's hall. Framed by bus windows as they inched through the cheering, tumultuous crowds. The Lincoln Memorial bathed in colored lights. The President praying simply, "Dear God, thank You! Thank You for what You've done!"

The days of celebration had all the thunder of a Fourth of July, all the dignity of an inauguration, and all the pathos of a reunion that had kept them hoping for fourteen months!

Americans had not been content to tie a yellow ribbon round an old oak tree. They tied them everywhere. On trees. On cars. On planes. On gates. On buildings. They tied one completely around the National Geographic Building. And the biggest yellow ribbon in history was tied in a bow round the Super Dome in New Orleans!

Yellow ribbons were everywhere. Canyons of yellow ribbons and flags and people slowed their buses almost to a stop. Miles and miles of ribbons—beside the highways and above them. Corridors of welcome they would never forget!

It all merged into a happy blur of color and tickertape and "God-bless-America" that was difficult to sort into days. But did it matter? It was crowding out the past, dimming the shouts of hate that had bombarded their ears those fourteen months, shrinking the memory of their ordeal to livable proportions. Said one former hostage, "It couldn't have been better if I had died and gone to heaven!"

Americans watched it all—from the streets and from their living rooms—and wept for joy. The hostages were home! They were safe! And not one of the fifty-two was lost!

But the captives haven't all come home. Probably you are aware that more and more reports are surfacing from individuals who claim that American servicemen, MIAs, are still being held, alive, in Vietnam—and in Laos. They have been seen in prisons, in camps, in chain gangs, at forced labor in the fields. It is said that some are held in caves. We ought to be praying that these, too, will come home!

Is the name Raoul Wallenberg familiar to you? He has been called "the lost hero of the holocaust." He was a young Swedish diplomat who, on a hot July day in 1944, arrived in Budapest on a mission that some say makes him the greatest hero of World War II. He was shy, soft-spoken, a member of an illustrious Swedish family. But he is credited with saving as many as 100,000 Hungarian Jews from extermination by the Nazis!

He accomplished this largely by issuing thousands of Swedish passports which he used to get Jews off the trains bound for the gas chambers, and to get them out of the long death marches to the Austrian border. Then he purchased or rented safe houses which flew the Swedish flag and sheltered Jews. The passports were actually worthless; but in the confusion and turmoil of war they worked!

The tragedy is that Wallenberg, at the end of the war, was arrested by troops of an Allied nation as a U.S. spy and has not been heard from since!

But it is reported anonymously that as late as 1980 he was alive, still a hostage, held in cell 77 of a certain well-known prison!

California congressman Tom Lantos and his wife Annette both credit Wallenberg with saving their lives when they were teenagers. And Lantos says, "I don't want to minimize the trauma of the fifty-two American hostages. But it is possible [that his captors] have kept him in anticipation of some meaningful exchange, and that Wallenberg is the ultimate hostage."

Yes, the hostages haven't all come home! And the truth is that some of them, at this moment, are reading these words!

Jesus said, "I tell you the truth, everyone who sins is a slave to sin." John 8:34, NIV.

Sin enslaves. It enslaves everyone it touches. And no man is more enslaved than the man who cannot see his own chains!

But Jesus came to free the captives of sin. See Luke 4:18. The chains that have bound you, that have left your life wounded and scarred, that have weakened your will, that have promised you freedom while they made you a slave—those shackles can be broken. They can be broken *now!*

Every one of us can be free from the *power* of sin, from its domination in our lives—if we choose. Says the apostle Paul, "Sin shall not have dominion over you." Romans 6:14, KJV.

But this does not mean that we are free from the *presence* of sin—sin in our environment. We are still surrounded by it, by its deceptive philosophy, and by the ruin and devastation it is causing in human lives.

We are still in enemy territory. From this point of view, every human being alive today is a hostage. This planet is still occupied by the forces of rebellion that took it over in the early morning of its history. Still held by the fallen angel who is the author of rebellion—and by the host of angels-turned-demons who chose to join him in his war against God. We are still here—for now. In that sense we are all still hostages.

The saddest day in all the history of the universe was the day the father of our race sold out to rebellion and made us all vulnerable to its infection.

Think, if you will—try to imagine—how God must have felt, how our Creator must have felt, the day it happened. It will break your heart. It broke His!

He knew what He would do. Calvary even then lay hidden in His heart. But in the meantime how could He let us know He cared? How could He let us know that the fallen angel's charges were untrue?

He sent us message after message. But the enemy did his best to jam the communication lines and to censor and distort and misinterpret the word that did get through. God sent us a long letter, full of love and assurance. But few bothered to read it.

Finally He sent His own Son to live among us. For thirty-three years He was hounded and harrassed and tempted by the enemy—just as we are hounded and harrassed and tempted. Then He was stretched upon a despised Roman cross and let men nail Him there—to die in our place, to die the death that should have been ours!

Love had found a way of getting through!

And then Jesus went back to His Father's house. But He left us with this promise: "Set your troubled hearts at rest. Trust in God always; trust also in me. There are many dwelling-places in my Father's house; if it were not so I should have told you; for I am going there on purpose to prepare a place for you. And if I go and prepare a place for you, I shall come again and receive you to myself, so that where I am you may be also." John 14:1-3, NEB.

A place for you. A place for me. What a promise! Not a filmy fiction on the edge of some cloud. Not a storyland. Not a dream world. *A place* as real as your own backyard. *A place* in God's country where you can build a house—and plant a vineyard. See Isaiah 65:21, 22. *A place* in the city that God has built. See Hebrews 11:10. *A place* in a city so real that it has foundations and walls and gates and streets and measurements. See Revelation 21:10-27.

A place where the blind will see, and the deaf will hear, and the dumb will sing (Isaish 35:5, 6)—and where no one will ever say, "I am sick" (Isaiah 33:24). *A place* where there is no pain or sorrow or death, where God Himself will wipe the tears from our eyes. See Revelation 21:4. And when God wipes away the tears, they will be gone forever!

But it has been quite a while now—since all this was promised. And some are saying that He doesn't care after all, that He has forgotten us, abandoned us, that we are hostages forever.

It isn't true! But the Lord Jesus—while He waits a little longer, for reasons we will soon understand—still searches for ways to let us know we are not forgotten.

Does heaven have an old oak tree—a very old oak tree— about which God can tie a yellow ribbon? I like to think that the stars God has hung in space, flashing against the velvet night, are God's yellow ribbons!

Think what it would be without the stars! Think what it would be like to be orbiting alone in the blackness, wondering if there is anybody out there, wondering if anybody knows we're here, wondering if there really is anybody else but us.

Thank God it isn't that way! God knows we're here. He hasn't forgotten us. His lamps are all lighted. Waiting to welcome us home!

I am fascinated with the way Amahl, the crippled boy in Gian-Carlo Menotti's Christmas opera, *Amahl and the Night Visitor*, describes the night sky. Remember how he limps indoors shrieking with ecstasy, "Oh, Mother, come and see . . ."? Remember his words?

> Oh, Mother, you should go out and see!
> There's never been such a sky!
> Damp clouds have shined it
> And soft winds have swept it
> As if to make ready for a King's ball.
> All its lanterns are lit,
> All its torches are burning,
> And its dark floor
> Is shining like crystal.
> Hanging over our roof
> There is a star as large as a window,
> And the star has a tail,
> And it moves across the sky
> Like a chariot on fire.
> And his mother says wearily,
> Oh Amahl! When will you stop telling lies?
> All day long you wander about in a dream.
> Here we are with nothing to eat,

Not a stick of wood on the fire,
Not a drop of oil in the jug,
And all you do is worry your mother
With fairy tales.

Friend, it *isn't* a fairy tale! All God's lamps *are* lighted. And one day soon the Lord Jesus will make His way down through that star-studded processionway of the skies to keep His promise. And not one hostage who wants to go home will be forgotten!

I think of the heroes of Vietnam who had reason to ask, "Where are *our* yellow ribbons?" Some of them will never walk again—until Jesus comes to set things right. No wonder they felt abandoned and unloved!

But you *aren't* abandoned. You *are* loved. Ask someone to wheel you out under the stars or push your bed near a window. Look up at those brilliant lamps, twinkling in the distance. They are God's yellow ribbons, lavished across the night to tell you that He cares!

Jesus is coming soon! And not one will be missed who wants to go home, who chooses to be included in His mission of rescue. Tell Him you want to be on His list. His angels will find you, wherever you are. Languishing in hospitals. Held captive in caves. Wherever. Not one will be missed!

Don't ever think that God doesn't *want* you to come home! He does, friend! He does!

Some years ago a boy quarreled with his father and left home. He said, "You'll never see me again!"

Three years passed—three tough years. He wanted to go home, but he was afraid. Would his father let him come back? He wrote his mother, told her that he would be on a certain train as it passed the house. He asked her to hang something white in the yard if it was all right with his dad to come home.

He was nervous on the train—sat in one seat and then another. A minister noticed, and asked what was wrong. He told him. They rode along together as the boy looked out the window.

Suddenly he started up excitedly. "Look, sir, my house is just around the bend, beyond the hill. Will you please look for me, see if there is something white? I can't stand to look. If there isn't anything white—you look, please!"

The train lurched a bit as it made a slow curve, and the minister kept his eyes on the round of the hill. Then he forgot his dignity as he fairly shouted, "Look, son, look!"

There was the little farmhouse under the trees. But you could hardly see the house for white. It seemed that those lonely parents had taken every white sheet in the house, every bedspread, every tablecloth, even every handkerchief—everything they could find that was white—and hung them out on the clothesline and on the trees!

The boy paled. His lips quivered. He couldn't speak. He was out of the train before it had completely stopped at the water tank. The last his new friend saw of him—he was running up the hill as fast as his legs could carry him—toward the sheets that were fluttering in the wind, and *home*!

That's what God has done. He's hung out every star He had—in dazzling white—all over the sky!

I like to picture that great day—when all the hostages go home. What a procession it will be, with Jesus Himself leading the way! With harps and crowns and flashing suns! God's yellow ribbons everywhere—as the tumultuous songs of welcome echo from world to world!

I like to think that the fifty-two will be there—and the heroes of Vietnam. Jeremiah Denton and all the POWs. And the MIAs. The captives that Jesus came to set free. The slaves of drink and drugs and smoke and sin of every stripe. All forgiven—washed clean in the blood of the Lamb!

I like to think that Raoul Wallenberg will be there. And you. And you. And you! Because you *can* be—if you choose!

In all God's universe, from His grandest galaxy to the smallest atom, will beat one pulse of harmony. No note of discord will ever mar God's vast creation. No voice will ever say good-bye. No heart will ever break. God's children, hostage so long in an alien land, will be at home forever. And the cry of this lonely planet, with its symphony of tears, will be no more!

Dear Friend:

You have just finished reading this brief but important resume of the fascinating book of Revelation. If you find a new concern developing, I earnestly hope you will proceed with further study of the Bible—especially the Revelation of Jesus, which reveals "the things which shall shortly come to pass." Several opportunities for continuing in-depth study of the Revelation are available to you.

First, you will find a description of two very helpful volumes on the inside back cover of this book—*God Cares,* volumes 1 and 2. Volume 1 explores the book of Daniel, and volume 2 is an explanation of Revelation. The books are scholarly but easy to read and understand. They will make deeper Bible study warm and appealing.

Second, Revelation Seminars are being conducted by "It Is Written" representatives in all areas of North America and in many countries overseas. Let me know of your interest, and I will do my best to acquaint you with the nearest seminar location.

And finally, I have recently completed thirty easy-to-understand video-cassette Bible studies. They are designed to cover the essential messages of Revelation as they relate to the entire Bible. The studies are entitled "Truth for the End Time." Just contact my office for further information on this series.

God bless you richly in your earnest search for truth. I am confident that you will not be disappointed as you study to know Him better, whom to know is life eternal—the Lord Jesus Christ, my Friend and your Friend.

Faithfully,
George E. Vandeman

It Is Written
Box 0,
Thousand Oaks, California 91360